"ABSORBING."
—*Esquire*

"Well-written, nonjudgmental, informative . . . [*Brothel*] could serve as a light at the end of a very long tunnel, and form the basis of both moral and legal discussions about prostitution in the future." —M. JOYCELYN ELDERS, M.D.

"A complex and all-too-human study . . . The result of this exhaustive and surprisingly compassionate research is a document that reads like a cross between a voyeuristic pulp novel and a thoroughly professional, not to mention essential, contribution to the annals of public health." —*The Baltimore Sun*

"Albert's Candide-like approach—an ingenuousness that characterizes the whole book and is by turns refreshing and somewhat incredible in our sex-besotted culture—enlivens the material, as does her tale of befriending Mustang women. . . . Albert gets us wondering about a lot of things, including our own reactions to this most naked and mysterious of transactions." —*Elle*

"Eye-opening . . . Albert writes in a simple, straightforward method, recounting conversations and incidents with ease and wit. . . . *Brothel* is far from sleazy. In fact it's an interesting read even if you oppose legalized prostitution and may even change your mind." —*Metro West Daily News* (MA)

"Engrossing . . . Albert convincingly dispels myths about this mysterious world and provides a strong defense for the legalization of prostitution." —*Publishers Weekly*

Please turn the page for more reviews. . . .

"A JAW-DROPPING SAGA."
—*The Sunday Times* (London)

"Colorful and sharply observed . . . A thorough and compassionate report on how prostitution is practiced in the only state where it's legal. . . . But it's Albert's attitude toward her topic, a mixture of emotions that average readers can identify with, that makes *Brothel* so readable."
—*Minneapolis Star Tribune*

"An empathetic portrait of women who sell sex for a living . . . An eye-opening look at their daily work routing and the way it affects the rest of their lives." —*Book* magazine

"Absorbing . . . [Albert] doesn't offer a romanticized vision of brothel life, but you very well might finish this book with newfound respect for hookers." —*New York Post*

"[Albert is] a smart, savvy, and articulate woman. . . . She could become one of the most outspoken people on the subject of sex and public health of her generation." —*Seattle Weekly*

"*Brothel* is the best kind of accessible sociology—full of empathy, detail, and the unique perspective of an outsider who got deep inside." —*nerve.com*

"[Albert] compassionately and insightfully discusses the prejudice prostitutes face even in places where prostitution is legal, and she shatters many common misconceptions . . . and avoids the stereotypes and feminist rhetoric to candidly depict legalized prostitution and its effect on the women involved in it."
—*Booklist*

Brothel

Brothel

Mustang Ranch and Its Women

ALEXA ALBERT

Ballantine Books • New York

A Ballantine Book

Published by The Ballantine Publishing Group

Ballantine and colophon are

registered trademarks of Random House, Inc.

www.ballantinebooks.com

Library of Congress Catalog Card Number: 2002090384

ISBN 0-449-00658-1

This edition published by arrangement with Random House, Inc.

Cover photo: Mustang Ranch © 1986/Timothy Hursley

Manufactured in the United States of America

First Ballantine Books Edition: July 2002

10 9 8 7 6 5 4 3 2 1

In *memory* of my friend Alfred

In *appreciation* of my husband, Andy,

and my father, Marvin

In *celebration* of my mother, Judy,

and my daughter, Coco

All the events that take place in this book are true. Because brothel prostitution in Nevada is still a very stigmatized business (despite its legal status) and most licensed prostitutes and their customers conceal their practices from loved ones, I have changed individuals' names and certain recognizable physical features to protect their identities.

CONTENTS

Brothel

1 .. THE OPENING

The postmark read "Reno Nevada, 24 Dec 1992." I stared at the envelope for a long moment before opening it. Reno? My mind was blank. Then it came to me: the brothel. For three and a half years, off and on, I had tried to convince a man named George Flint, executive director of the Nevada Brothel Association, to grant me permission to conduct a research study inside Nevada's legal brothels, the only licensed houses of prostitution in America. My letters and telephone calls had been for naught; Flint stood firm that the brothel industry wasn't available for a researcher's examination. "Brothel people are very private people," he had told me. "They don't like people nosing around."

It had become a ritual to send him a card every year reminding him of my project. I had long ago stopped entertaining any serious hope that he would agree, so I was in a slight daze when I tore open the envelope and read: "Your holiday card arrived earlier today. There may come a time that we can do something substantive together. Call me sometime and we will talk. George Flint."

I FIRST BEGAN to think seriously about Nevada's legal brothels in 1989. I was an undergraduate and fascinated by public health issues; the AIDS crisis had exploded into mainstream public consciousness; and prostitution was the focus of national attention as public health officials hotly contested the role of sex workers in the transmission of HIV. In the context of that debate, I had learned that certain areas of Nevada licensed brothel prostitution, with specific ordinances established to safeguard the health and safety of the public. These controls were said to greatly reduce the dangers typically associated with street prostitution—violent crime, drug use, and disease transmission. Latex condoms were required for all brothel sexual activity, and women were tested regularly for sexually transmitted diseases, including HIV. Since HIV testing began in 1986, no brothel worker had tested positive, I was told, and the incidence of other STDs was negligible.

Before I could reckon with the public health implications of this information, I had to get over my astonishment that one of our culture's great taboos was legally sanctioned by one (and only one) American state. Why was this fact never made a national issue? What about the women? Prostitution carries with it a grave stigma; did being licensed and legal diminish that? Did legality assure these women legitimacy, even a sense of professionalism? The more I considered the human questions, the more they came to haunt me, and I found growing within me a desire to get inside this world and understand it. That the brothels were strictly off-limits to non-"working" women only goaded me further.

That summer, I took an internship in family planning and human sexuality at Emory University that required me to develop a public health study. After a lot of thought and much grief from my family and fiancé, I submitted a proposal to investigate brothel prostitutes' condom-use practices. Hard data on the efficacy of condom use in preventing HIV infection was scarce, and the issue was complicated by the very real problem of condom slippage and breakage. That hundreds of women in Nevada should be having multiple sexual partners every day without any reported HIV transmission was almost too good to be true. If I could verify it, and learn exactly what the women were doing right, I had a chance, I felt, to accomplish something important. I thought the brothels would surely cooperate with the project: it offered society valuable public health information, and it gave them validation as safe and responsible businesses.

My naïveté was rubbed in my face when George Flint point-blank refused me entry. At least I wasn't the only one; after doing a little more research, I realized how few outsiders had ever been permitted to investigate the brothel industry in any real depth. Prostitutes were kept on the premises behind locked electric gates, and visitors were surveilled before being buzzed in. Media coverage was very controlled; the brothels had been featured a few times on television programs like *Donahue, Geraldo,* and *Jerry Springer,* but the audience was shown only the most superficial aspects of the business.

Needless to say, my astonishment was total when Flint wrote me three and a half years later to invite me to Nevada to conduct my research project on condom-use practices. Certainly, the project was still valid, and at this point in my life I was in the process of applying to medical school and planning my wedding. I was put on guard, though, by something he said when we spoke by phone: "Anything positive that comes from a prestigious place like Emory helps to support our cause." Was that what my study was doing? Was he in dire straits suddenly and desperate for PR? If so, did I want to help? Did I want to support brothel owners and promote the expansion of legalized prostitution in America? While I was curious to see whether legalized brothels actually provided prostitutes with more protection than illegal prostitution, I fundamentally believed prostitution was a dehumanizing, objectifying business that did women real damage. Was I being roped into being its booster?

Flint went on to say, "It's not going to be like breezing in and counting tomatoes or comparing prices in a grocery store. The working ladies are very private people. They don't trust outsiders. You're in for a real education, honey." Suddenly, the study I'd written off was a reality, and my mind began to race. Absent any more information, nightmare scenarios multiplied. Who were these women who allowed themselves to be locked behind gates? Were they all drug addicts and survivors of heinous sexual abuse, like so many street prostitutes? Were they chained to beds, as prostitutes allegedly were in Thailand? Would they even agree to speak with me? Above all, did I have it in me to do this? Yes, I decided. I bought a plane ticket.

My family didn't help. They were even more uncomfortable than I was. As long as I wasn't allowed inside, my interest in the project had been entertaining. But now I was headed to Nevada, and suddenly my parents wondered why I was so interested in an underworld teeming with criminals and degenerates. My future in-laws were even more confused. Let us get this straight: You're choosing to leave our son for an entire month to conduct research in a *brothel*? Do you secretly desire to become a prostitute? What are we going to tell our friends? Andy, my husband-to-be, had his own worries, my physical safety not the least among them.

In the end, apprehension and all, I made that flight to Reno. Awaiting me at the Reno airport was a man named Marty who had been sent to pick me up and deliver me to Flint at a place called Chapel of the Bells. Flint was not only executive director of the Nevada Brothel Association, I learned, but a (retired) ordained minister as well. In fact, he owned one of Reno's twelve wedding chapel businesses—and arguably the nicest, or at least the only freestanding one. (The others were storefronts.) With its whitewashed façade, faux stained-glass windows, and prominent cupola, Flint's Chapel of the Bells looked more like Disney's version of the gingerbread house in "Hansel and Gretel" than a wedding chapel.

In the lobby, white lace-print paper lined the walls and a pattern of miniature flowers decorated the ceiling moldings like frosting on a wedding cake. An assortment of bridal bouquets, boutonnières, garter belts, and champagne flutes was showcased for newlyweds who wanted such traditional wedding frills. On the walls hung sobering certificates and plaques that authenticated George Flint's maternal ancestors, the Treats, as descendants of the founders of New Jersey and Connecticut. Flint would later tell me that he could trace his family's lineage all the way back to Charlemagne.

While I waited for my audience with Flint, I watched a live feed on a closed-circuit television of a wedding in progress. A female minister was presiding over the marriage of a middle-aged Frenchman to a diminutive and considerably younger-looking Vietnamese bride who clearly spoke much less English than he did, which is to say, almost none.

Finally Flint appeared. For nearly four years, I'd wondered what the brothel industry's gatekeeper looked like. A flashy, gum-smacking, middle-aged street hustler with a cockeyed hairpiece and several heavy gold necklaces buried in dark chest hair is what I had expected. Instead, I saw a man in his early sixties, of ample proportions and intense civility. He wore tinted eyeglasses, and several expensive—but not gaudy—rings flashed from thick fingers. He wobbled a little as he walked, because of a serious leg injury. He looked safer, friendlier, and more polished than I'd imagined. I couldn't help but see in my mind's eye a smiling Midwestern televangelist wooing an admiring and loving audience.

As he led me down to his basement office, he peppered me with unexpected questions about my family. Did I know my ancestry, he asked? Did I have any interest in genealogy? I admitted I hadn't given it much thought—certainly not as much as he had. He told me about each of the family portraits hanging on the basement walls. His father had been a professional photographer and Flint confessed that he had inherited his passion for photography from his dad. In fact, George—he insisted I call him George rather than Mr. Flint or Reverend Flint—admitted to many passions, from travel and antiques to Napoleon and the embalming practices of morticians. I found myself nodding pleasantly and in half-disbelief as his stories rolled over me, delivered in the soothing cadences of a professional preacher.

Suddenly, George changed the subject. "Why is it that women who were sexually aggressive before marriage, never want to give a guy oral sex after they're married?" Did he expect me to answer that? George didn't need an answer. The problem, he explained, lay in our society's inability to communicate about sex. Men fundamentally wanted to be monogamous, he contended, but resorted to having affairs or going to brothels when they felt uncomfortable discussing their sexual fantasies with their wives. Then, warming to his other job as brothel lobbyist, he began to tick off a litany of reasons for legalizing prostitution.

As he went on, passionately endorsing the sex trade from inside his wedding chapel, I couldn't help but wonder how he reconciled the two professions. Maybe he didn't need to; clearly he was a man comfortable with life's contradictions. With a wink or a sneer, he would proffer a story about the way the world worked, and about the weakness to which the flesh is heir. There was the one about the state senator who fell in love with a brothel prostitute after one night of passion and refused to let her leave the room. "Georgie, can't I keep her?" the senator had whined over the phone in the wee hours of the morning, according to George.

His utter candor, his vocal, affable openness, and his basically charming disposition were disarming, even endearing. And while his self-righteous rationalizations of the brothel trade were hardly unimpeachable, it was obvious that he had a genuine affection for the women—"the girls," as he called them.

The sun was setting as George and I finally drove out in his white Cadillac to Mustang Ranch. It was Nevada's largest, best-known, and most profitable brothel, accounting for nearly half of the $50 million in revenue produced by the state's licensed brothels each year. It was about twelve miles east of Reno, across the Washoe County line in Storey County. As we drove along Interstate 80, strip malls and neon lights fell away, replaced by a desert landscape painted in time-marked layers of reds, pinks, and browns. Near the exit for the brothel, we spotted a herd of wild horses, some of the mustangs for which the brothel was named. Exit 23 twisted down past a junkyard and under the Southern Pacific railroad tracks, then crossed the Truckee River on a one-lane bridge. There, on the fifty acres the locals called Happy Valley, or the Valley of the Dolls, out of sight of the highway, surrounded by low hills and scrub brush, was the Mustang Ranch.

I suppose I envisioned the sort of mid-Victorian New Orleans whorehouse I'd seen in movies like *Pretty Baby*, but Mustang Ranch was nothing of the sort. It consisted of two nondescript buildings a hundred yards apart, separated by a parking lot big enough to hold a hundred cars and a dozen eighteen-wheelers. Spanish-style wrought-iron gates enclosed each building, with its little plot of grass in front. I was reminded of a pitch-and-putt miniature-golf castle. Mustang #1 faced the road head on: a pink stucco building with a red tile roof. A huge illuminated pink sign with the Mustang logo—an illustration of a woman's face—hung over the gate. Behind the building stood a twenty-four-foot lookout tower, a relic of a time when Mustang's founder, Joe Conforte, had erected a pair of them to defend his enterprise. I would later learn that after the murder of a heavyweight boxer named Oscar Bonavena at Mustang, the tower by the parking lot, from which some say the bullet was fired, was torn down. The remaining tower, behind the brothel, stood ominous and unused.

George drove past Mustang #1 and pulled up in front of Mustang #2, a smaller building whose dark-stained exterior blended more inconspicuously into the desert background. We were buzzed in through the electric gate and greeted coldly at the front door by the "floor maid," or hostess. "George, you know you can't bring ladies in here," she snapped. George explained wearily that I was here as an invited guest of the Nevada Brothel Association to conduct some research. The woman's gaze softened slightly. Nothing personal, George later told me: the industry had adopted a firm no-woman policy to put a stop to the domestic disputes that broke out, disrupting business, when wives and girlfriends came looking for their partners.

I tried to glance nonchalantly around the room, as if it were nothing out of the ordinary for me to be in a brothel. A jukebox blared out the Foreigner song "Hot Blooded" from the center of the room, in front of a partition that divided the parlor area from the bar behind. Against the walls sat several black velvet sofas and a cigarette machine. Neon beer signs and an assortment of Mustang Ranch T-shirts and windbreakers for sale decorated the walls above the bar. The lights were kept dim, and the room felt like a seedy biker bar, minus only a pool table and a pinball machine. On my left, a young black woman with seductive but disengaged eyes sprawled across one of the couches. Another woman strode across the parlor in spiked heels, smoking a cigarette. An Asian man in a 49ers sweatshirt chatted quietly with a redhead on another sofa.

Slow Monday night, George remarked. He walked away to speak with management about my visit, leaving me at the bar to take in the environment. The three women in the room stared at me for a few minutes, but their interest eventually dwindled and I was left alone. George reappeared after about twenty minutes and surprised me with an invitation to stay at the Ranch so as to be close to the subjects of my study. *Live* inside the brothel? I hesitated. I had planned to stay in a cheap Reno motel, never expecting an opportunity like this. My head spun. Sensing my ambivalence, George assured me he'd check in regularly. I took a deep breath. No half measures, Alexa. I moved in that evening.

THAT FIRST NIGHT, I lay in bed listening to the doorbell ring continuously, announcing the arrival of male visitors. I had been given a vacant room down Hallway B, what was called the night girls' hallway. My neighbors all worked the shift from eleven P.M. to eleven A.M. Because of the brothel's narrow hallways, no wider than four feet, and thin walls, prostitutes' rooms were typically clustered by shifts so that off-duty women could sleep undisturbed. I could hear a woman's moans through the rice-paper wall at the head of my bed. For a moment, I was alarmed: Was someone hurt? Then I reminded myself where I was, and tried to figure out whether these were sounds of genuine pleasure. I couldn't tell. Every few minutes, her customer emitted a rough grunt and occasionally they both laughed. I couldn't help but think that the sounds the man was making were deeply unarousing; I tried to imagine being forced to act pleasured by some man I didn't know making guttural animal sounds, and I couldn't. At least I felt relatively safe, though I did have fleeting fears of awakening in the middle of the night to find a drunken man groping at my nightgown. (Although I'd locked my door, I was sure the push-button lock was easy to pick.) I closed my eyes tight and let the thoughts pass. I had nowhere else to go.

The next day, I began interviewing women, with the help of Irene, Mustang #2's manager. Irene had been at Mustang for two years. Unlike most brothel managers, she hadn't been a prostitute. She had come to Mustang as a "square," as prostitutes called those outside the sex industry. She took a job as a cashier four months after her husband's death. Three months later, she was promoted to manager. She was a short, squat woman in her late fifties. Her matronly physique contrasted with a crass tongue and a gruff cigarette-scarred voice. She had seen her share of hard times, she told me, and believed it was just happenstance that she herself hadn't become a working girl. An unwed teen mother in the 1950s, she had married a man she never loved to escape her mother's house. During the 1960s, she worked at a racetrack in Philadelphia; there she had her first exposure to prostitutes and started a love affair with a married *Philadelphia Tribune* sportswriter. Eventually she married him and they lived happily together for twenty-two years, until his untimely death at the age of sixty-five.

Her lack of experience in the sex industry had made her timid, even fearful, during her first months as cashier, Irene confided. Rather than mingle with the girls or customers, she kept to herself and stayed inside her cashier's cage. But the loneliness of recent widowhood drove her to seek connections with the prostitutes, many of whom seemed as solitary and abandoned as she felt. Quickly, Irene became Mustang #2's den mom, attending to the women's needs and judiciously doling out hugs and discipline.

Irene made it perfectly clear at the outset that she was the prostitutes' advocate. She wanted the women to understand clearly the purpose of my study before they agreed to participate. To give the women some privacy, she allowed me to use her office for interviews. With her support, and the $40 cash I promised each woman upon the study's completion, most of the prostitutes at #2 agreed to participate.

My first subject was Star, a young black woman dressed in a turquoise spandex bodysuit. She had long, straightened hair and ebony skin that was smooth save for one small raised scar over her left breast, from a cigarette burn many years earlier. As she walked into the office, she immediately made her reservations known. "I can't waste no time back here. I have to earn some money." I proceeded tentatively, glancing her way anxiously whenever the doorbell rang to announce a customer. In spite of herself, however, Star seemed to enjoy the interview and actually looked surprised when we finished nearly forty-five minutes later. A look of consternation crossed her face as I explained the next phase of the study.

"You want me to save the rubbers?" she asked, incredulous.

When I tried to explain that I needed to examine the condoms for breaks, her eyes glazed over and she cut me off. "Just so long as I get my forty bucks at the end."

I interviewed five more women that first day. Though very different in appearance, all were surprisingly attractive, I found myself thinking, from a buxom Native American with silky-smooth black hair to her waist and bloodred fingernails, to a bleached blonde with serpent tattoos spiraling up her calves. I guess I had expected to find only tough, hard-looking women. Many of Mustang's women could have been mistaken for beauticians or department-store cosmetic saleswomen. There were even a few women whose endowments and overt sexuality suggested a centerfold, the American sexual gold standard: Ashley, for instance, a statuesque working girl in her early twenties who wore a sheer black peignoir trimmed with lush marabou over a rhinestone-studded black bikini and matching black marabou slippers.

At the end of my first day, I felt relieved not to have offended anyone with my questions. Irene invited me to join her and Roxanne, the laundry maid, for dinner. I followed them into the brothel kitchen, a large open room with industrial refrigerators and a large stainless-steel restaurant stove. Cliff, the brothel cook, had prepared a buffet of warm dishes. I took some homemade fried chicken and a baked potato, and Irene chose barbecued ribs and collard greens. We carried our plates over to one of the six tables covered in plastic red-and-white-checked tablecloths scarred with cigarette burns. I was struck by how good the food was. Working girls continuously interrupted our meal to gripe to Irene about a customer who'd failed to tip them or a colleague who borrowed and mistreated an outfit. In between complaints, Irene and Roxanne groused about specific girls who copped princess attitudes and refused to clean up after themselves.

That night I fell into bed exhausted, almost too tired to hear the sounds of sex coming through my bedroom walls. I wondered how much of my fatigue came from the shock of the new, and how much was due to the brothel's poor ventilation and ubiquitous cigarette smoke.

The next two days, I woke early and continued interviewing women. By now, everyone in the house—from working girls to cashiers and bartenders—knew I was George Flint's guest, a researcher from a university who wanted the women to save their used condoms. Occasionally, staff members would come up to me to ask what I planned to do with the condoms. I got the sense that some of them thought I had a fetish.

As the women became more accustomed to me, they grew

friendlier. At first, they approached only to recount stories about collecting the condoms. One woman described how her client had wanted his used condom to be recognizable, so they had tied it up with a red ribbon. Another apologized because she hadn't yet collected all ten condoms for which I'd asked; she had only had six "dates."

When I wasn't interviewing, I tried to keep a low profile, and hid out in the kitchen or television room, listening to the doorbell ringing in the parlor. I wasn't sure whether brothel management would permit me to sit in the parlor among the women and clients. Would my presence seem disruptive? Would I distract the women from their business? What if a client approached me? Staying out seemed the best way to assure not wearing out my welcome. Still, I couldn't help being curious.

Irene must have picked up on this, for on my third night she invited me to join her at the bar and offered me a seat with good visibility of the parlor so I could watch as men came through the front door. The drill was remarkably systematized. To gain admittance, clients rang a bell on the electrically controlled outside gate. Before being buzzed inside, they were surveyed by the cashier or floor maid in the daytime, by a security guard at night. Men who appeared drunk, rowdy, or underage were denied entry.

By the time men reached the front door after walking up a sixty-foot pathway, women had arranged themselves in a lineup in the center of the parlor. Customers were greeted by the spectacle of twenty or thirty women of all shapes and sizes and in various degrees of undress, standing at attention like a row of X-rated Barbie dolls. "Welcome to Mustang Ranch, sir," said the floor maid, who greeted men at the front door. "These are the ladies available to you. Ladies, please introduce yourselves."

One by one, the women went down the line offering their working names, aliases such as Bambi, Fancy, and Champagne. On cursory inspection, most of the women appeared pleasant, smiling cordially but reticently, in compliance with house rules. A few dared to flirt more candidly, teasing with a sly wink or flashing a coquettish glance. On closer examination, the women's eyes revealed more genuine feelings: annoyance, indifference, desperation, disdain, agitation, and occasionally intoxication.

The customers didn't seem to notice. They were simply too stunned. Some communicated their astonishment with awkward exclamations: "Holey moley!" "Wow, what a spread!" The dramatic ones staggered backward; a few even clutched their chests. One astonished man dressed in a cotton jersey and sneakers stood motionless and asked, "What do I do?"

"You choose, honey," said the floor maid. It was her responsibility to shepherd along baffled customers.

Finally, after scrutinizing the women for a few seconds, he pointed nervously to one on the far right, at the end of the lineup. "The animal print outfit," he exclaimed. Like many other customers overwhelmed by the formation, he had failed to catch the women's names.

Many seemed to get stuck on this detail. "Can they do that again? Say their names again?" asked a balding man in his forties, dressed in a red polo shirt, khakis, and leather loafers. The floor maid maintained her hospitable smile, but furrowed her eyebrows to indicate that she had no intention of making the women stand on display a minute longer. When the man still didn't pick, she shrugged and gave a nod to the women to disband.

Irene remarked that the floor maid on duty that night was strong on sales and peddling the merchandise. Instead of asking customers *if* they would like to select a lady, she asked, "*Which* lady would you like to select?" When a customer opted for a drink at the bar instead, she pitched hard, telling him that any woman of his choosing would be more than willing to serve him drinks in her room. I watched as several men submitted under such pressure. (Unlike Nevada's so-called parlor houses, Mustang was a bar house, which meant customers didn't have to select immediately from the lineup but could opt first for a drink at the bar. After downing some liquid courage, however, customers were expected to choose a prostitute. To that end, women one by one approached the barflies and tried to lure them back to their rooms.)

Once a man picked a woman, he followed her back to her room to negotiate a "party." Most customers settled upon a price, which usually ranged between $150 and $500 ("fantasy sessions" cost more), depending on the time of day, the day of the week, the customer's attitude, and how drunk or high he was. Mustang accepted cash and most credit cards, but not American Express, which refused to service houses of ill repute, legal or otherwise. An innocuous, unincriminating company name appeared on the invoice; at Mustang it said Nevada Novelties, Inc. There was even an ATM in Mustang's parlor, in case customers ran out of cash. Customers who couldn't reach an agreement on price with a prostitute got "walked," or escorted back to the front parlor, where they were free to negotiate with a different working girl. With an average of six customers per day, prostitutes earned $300 to $1,500 daily.

As the staff grew more comfortable with my presence over the next couple of days, they permitted me to roam throughout Mustang #2 as I pleased. I spent hours on the parlor sofas watching the lineup, entertaining myself by silently handicapping each woman, asking myself who was most eye-catching, or whose outfit was most shameless. Was it the wet-pink vinyl, lace-up cat suit, or the sheer, sapphire baby doll? Over time, I learned to read the women's facial expressions and could pick out who looked most desperate for a customer and who was avoiding eye contact with a client in the hopes of not being picked.

I also got good at identifying each woman's particular way of greeting a customer once she was picked from the lineup. Tilly made physical contact immediately, either offering an outstretched hand to shake or, more aggressively, grabbing the man's arm and leading him back to her room. In contrast, some of the newer girls, like Samantha and Amy, gave every customer the same forced smile before turning on their heels and heading back to their rooms, the men following silently like puppy dogs.

On my fifth day, I finished interviewing all the women at Mustang #2 who met the study's eligibility criteria. It was time for me to venture over to Mustang #1 to enroll more women. But I dreaded the prospect. By now, I had picked up bits and pieces of gossip about the other house. According to the working girls at #2, the prostitutes at #1 could be vicious. Mustang #1 tended to be full of experienced working girls known to be competitive, stuck-up, and insolent; Mustang #2 got more of the turn-outs—the first-time working girls—who helped to make the place more hospitable and neighborly.

Although they were under the same ownership, Mustang Ranch's two compounds had always differed considerably, it seemed. Larger and more opulent, Mustang #1 was considered the main house, #2 merely an annex; it had been built in 1984 to handle #1's overflow. Rumor had it that Joe Conforte used to put all his girlfriends over at #2, safe and out of sight of Sally, his wife, who managed both houses from her suite at #1.

With trepidation, I headed over to #1, where Vivian, the manager, greeted me. Vivian had been in the business off and on for over thirty years, first as one of Joe Conforte's working girls in the late 1960s and throughout the 1970s. Fifty-four years old, she was an attractive, slender woman with high cheekbones and a mane of auburn hair that she had the habit of swinging from side to side. She quickly led me through the kitchen—twice the size of Mustang #2's—and back to an office, where she informed me that I could expect "excellent" participation from her girls. If anyone gave me trouble, I was to contact her. Unlike Irene, Vivian had simply announced she expected all of the prostitutes to participate if they wanted to stay her girls. They needed to give something back, she explained, for the privilege of working in a legal house.

Vivian sent women back one by one to be interviewed; indeed, they immediately struck me as different from the women in Mustang #2. Although most were polite, they seemed impenetrable, aloof. Tanya, an older brunette who barely cracked a smile, asked me with thinly veiled disdain who I really thought cared about the condom information I was collecting. She had never had a condom break or slip off, and frankly, there wasn't much else to say. Later in the afternoon, another woman informed me that some of her friends didn't like the way I had phrased certain questions. Do you think we're stupid? she asked. Is that why I'd used the expression "come" instead of "orgasm"? Still, I managed to complete six interviews my first day at #1 and to convince all six women to continue with the study—although Tanya made it clear, "Like I've already told you, I don't break condoms."

Despite Vivian's civil reception, the staff, too, was more hostile. I had barely glanced into Mustang #1's parlor—a large octagonal room with a two-story vaulted ceiling, skylights, scarlet wall-to-wall carpeting, and eight hallways extending out to the women's bedrooms like spokes on a wagon wheel—when I was accosted by a floor maid named Shelley, a woman my age who wore oversized plastic-framed glasses and had her hair pulled back in a tight ponytail. (I later learned that she had been a working girl at Mustang several years before, and that she had specialized in sadism.) "You're the one asking questions," she barked, her cold eyes piercing mine. I nodded, assuming she meant my research questions. "Well, you can't be in here," she continued. "You don't belong here." "Here" was the parlor, but deep down, I suspected, she really meant the brothel. Effectively bullied, I apologized and asked her to tell Vivian I would be back in the morning.

As I rushed across the parking lots dividing Mustang #1 from #2, the fresh, balmy desert air touched my skin, and it hit me that until today, I had spent the past five days entirely indoors at #2. Every day through the windows I had noticed the sun sparkling off the sagebrush-speckled hills, but I hadn't thought much of the fact that I hadn't been outside. On a few occasions, I had caught sight of a carload of tourists posing outside the brothel fence for a photo, and it had struck me that the brothel residents actually lived like animals in a zoo. The gates that surrounded most of Nevada's brothels were supposedly built to protect prostitutes, staff, and customers alike from outside provocation. But whereas the non-"working" staff and the customers were at liberty to come and go, the working girls were required to remain on the premises and were let out for fresh-air breaks only in the enclosed front and back yards. (At management's discretion, they could occasionally take twenty-four- and forty-eight-hour leaves from the brothel.)

As soon as I entered Mustang #2, the women greeted me enthusiastically, eager to hear about the other house. I appreciated their warmth and attentiveness after my frosty treatment at #1. The new turn-outs wanted to know how beautiful the women at #1 were. Those who had been fired from #1 and were doing their time on probation at #2 wanted to know whether their friends (and enemies) were still working there.

Their reception made me realize what a welcome diversion I'd been for them. Instead of disturbing the normal flow of their business, I was the source of much amusement. I was teased relentlessly for my squareness and frequently made the butt of their jokes. One evening, a couple of women sent a client over to proposition me after telling him I was cheap—real cheap. "She'll only charge you twenty," I overheard one woman say. At that time, the house minimum for any sexual activity was $60 (later raised to $100). The women doubled over on their bar stools in hysterics. Confused by the women's laughter, the mousy-looking man who now stood before me faltered. I had to explain I didn't work at Mustang.

That wasn't the first time I had been approached by a customer. With my conservative attire and the notebook and pen I carried with me religiously, I tried to stay visibly distinguishable from the working girls. I didn't always succeed. One night a Mexican man who had been guzzling Budweisers with his buddies for over two hours came over and perched himself on the bar stool next to mine. "I know you like me," he said, his breath reeking of alcohol. "I want to make love to you. My friend have money. Much money."

He suddenly became unsteady on his seat and grabbed hold of the bar to regain his balance. The next thing I knew, he subtly slid his arm behind me and groped my right breast. My mouth dropped. I looked around, but no one had seen him grab me; the women were in the middle of a lineup, Irene was filling in as floor maid, and the bartender was serving another customer. This man obviously felt entitled to cop a feel because he was in a brothel. Would he ever have tried that move in a squares' bar? What was a prostitute in his eyes?

After I informed him I wasn't a working girl, he started apologizing profusely. He felt ashamed at having taken me for a prostitute. He obviously judged prostitutes as intrinsically different from other women. I know I pitied the prostitutes for the men they ended up servicing. I stood in judgment of the johns, certain I would never freely choose to be intimately involved with a man who paid a stranger for sex. But, as angered as I was by the stereotyping of prostitutes, I had to admit that maybe the tricks, like the working girls, deserved to be better understood.

THE COOL RECEPTION I got at the main house changed soon after I met Baby. A slender, five-foot-eleven strawberry-blonde in her early forties who frequently wore her hair up in a French twist, Baby had worked on and off at Mustang Ranch since 1979. In addition to being one of Mustang's most seasoned prostitutes, she was also one of its most successful and well respected. Although she was a night girl and slept during the days, we seemed to cross paths constantly. We usually kept our greetings brief, but I detected a desire in her to linger and converse.

Then one day, Baby invited me to join her and another working girl at one of the kitchen tables. I did. As I sat down, Baby turned to me. How had my stay gone thus far? Was I learning a lot? Were the girls being nice? Since she had been the first to bother to ask, I decided to take the plunge and to speak frankly. I told her that the women at #2 had warmed up to me quicker, perhaps because that was where I was staying and spending most of my time.

"You should sit in our parlor here, too," Baby said firmly, unaware of Shelley's intimidation tactics. I detected a competitive edge in her voice. I already knew the women at #1 were used to being preferred over those at #2. Did she want me, the visiting outsider, to favor #1 as well? Baby hadn't seemed surprised to hear that her colleagues at #1 had been standoffish. She promised to see what she could do.

Over the next couple of days, two things happened. First, I decided to take Baby's advice and to venture over to #1 more frequently and with more courage. (I tried to ignore Shelley's glares.) Secondly, women at #1 became more gracious. A few let slip that Baby had spoken highly of me. Baby was their litmus paper; if she thought she could trust me, so could they. In the end, Baby greatly eased my entry into the community. And she not only smoothed the way for me with the others, but ultimately became my friend.

IN THE COURSE of my three-week study, I managed to collect a great deal of information.* Brothel prostitutes were com-

---

*Albert AE, Warner DL, Hatcher RA, Trussell J, Bennett C. Condom use among female commercial sex workers in Nevada's legal brothels. *American Journal of Public Health* 1995; 85: 1514–1520.

Albert AE, Warner DL, Hatcher RA. Facilitating condom use with clients during commercial sex in Nevada's legal brothels. *American Journal of Public Health* 1998; 88: 643–646.

plying with Nevada's mandatory condom law and using an average of six condoms per day with their customers. Not surprisingly, these women were expert condom users, and the rubbers rarely broke or slipped off. It seemed practice did make perfect. They explained their techniques to prevent condoms from breaking: they always insisted on putting the condom on the client themselves, and they frequently stopped sex to visually check the integrity of the condom. It wasn't uncommon for women to double up on condoms. Finally, when sex lasted a long time, women stopped to change condoms.

Although the AIDS epidemic was already a decade old, customers were still trying to persuade women not to use condoms. Some tried the classic excuses—that rubbers decreased sensation and prevented them from having an orgasm. Others came up with more original lines: "I've only been with my wife of thirty years"; "I'm a doctor." Some men told the women, "You get tested so I know you're clean." Did these customers think that women were insisting on condoms for the *men's* protection? It wasn't uncommon for men to offer women extra money or even try to slip the condom off during sex. Nevertheless, the women usually managed to transform the condom into an acceptable and even erotic part of sex—a skill that could be useful for other women, sex workers and non–sex workers alike.

A few of the women turned the tables on me. Did I use condoms with my fiancé? I started to say "No, we're monogamous," but caught myself and mumbled "No, but I probably ought to." According to these prostitutes, most of their customers were married, and I'm sure the men's wives hoped and believed, like me, that their significant others were faithful.

Despite their caution on the job, even the Mustang women rationalized not using condoms with their husbands and boyfriends, who they assumed were monogamous. At first I couldn't believe these women hadn't grown more cynical about marriage and monogamy, given the amount of infidelity they witnessed. Their hopefulness in spite of what they knew about human nature made my heart ache. These women were just like the rest of us.

All of which made me think: it was prostitutes and other sex workers whom we in mainstream America accused of contributing to the spread of HIV. Society blamed prostitutes' recklessness on ignorance, poverty, and disregard for personal responsibility, but I knew plenty of people who were more educated and more affluent and failed to properly protect themselves sexually. Despite widespread condom promotion by the mainstream media, my own friends neglected to use rubbers regularly with new partners. My future brother-in-law said he and his friends, all ten years my junior, worried more about pregnancy than disease. By contrast, Nevada's licensed prostitutes seemed remarkably conscientious. I wondered who really should be casting the first stone.

Relishing the opportunity to turn the magnifying glass on me, the prostitutes of Mustang Ranch wanted most to know if I could ever turn a trick. Because of my apparent interest in prostitution, they assumed that deep down I wanted to try. (I would discover that most people assumed the same thing.) Not wanting to offend anyone, I kept to myself how repulsive I found the idea. I tried to dodge the question by saying I didn't think I would make a very good prostitute.

But that was exactly where I—like all squares—was wrong, the working girls said. All women sold sex for one reason or another. The housewife who slept with her husband to maintain her household, the secretary who dated her boss for job security, the girlfriend who had sex with her boyfriend for status or another piece of jewelry (maybe an engagement ring). Prostitutes just did it more honestly. "My motto is, 'A bitch with a pussy should never be broke,'" one terse Mustang prostitute said. "If you're going to put out, why not get paid for it? There's too many women giving their bodies away for free and getting nothing but heartache and pain."

It was an argument I would hear used over and over again to defend brothel prostitution. Although I struggled with the notion that all sexual relationships could be reduced to commerce, the women's larger point wasn't wasted on me. Prostitutes weren't social deviants, they were trying to say. They were no different from other women.

All the working girls had stories about feeling disrespected and misunderstood. Baby once confessed to another American vacationer on a tour of Japan that she was a brothel prostitute; he ignored her for the rest of the trip. Her friend Barbie overheard a ticket agent in the Reno airport complain to her colleague about the brothels and how "those damn prostitutes" were a constant threat to her marriage.

Even I encountered the contempt Mustang prostitutes described when I went home four weeks later and tried to describe my experience to family and friends. People cared less about how decent and helpful the women were than about how much money they made, what types of sexual activities they sold, and what horrible circumstances forced them to resort to selling their bodies in the first place. Andy simply wanted reassurance I hadn't kissed anybody, and my younger cousin needed to know I hadn't become a prostitute. Perhaps my sister-in-law exemplified the general view best when she mistook my acknowledgment of the women as great condom experts and public health resources for approval of their work. "I just don't see how you can support prostitution," she said.

To be honest, I still wasn't sure how I felt about legalized prostitution. At the time, my head was spinning. I had long believed that prostitution represented "badness" on multiple levels. Practically, it disturbed me because of the dangers to the women who practiced it. Politically, I thought prostitution degraded all women. But Nevada's legal brothels were far less repugnant than I had expected. They appeared to be clean, legitimate workplaces, and the women were not shackled hostages but self-aware professionals there of their own free will.

Still, I knew so little. How had Nevada come to legalize brothel prostitution in the first place? How did one become a licensed prostitute? What drove individuals to abandon mainstream society to work in such isolation, in houses of prostitution? How did the women feel about the work they did and about each other? Who were their customers? Did their relationships with these men ever become more than professional?

How did other locals feel about the legal brothels and their prostitutes? How long did women do this work; was there ever an end?

I knew I needed to learn more about Nevada's brothel industry. These women's lives had moved me deeply, and the Mustang Ranch was an astonishingly rich environment for examining some of America's most loaded social issues.

Two years passed before I could return to Mustang Ranch, during the summer between my first and second years of medical school. I was delighted to discover that Baby and many of the other women I had met were still working there. Baby greeted me effusively, and we embraced like long-lost friends. She told me she'd suspected I would return. Then she confessed why she had first taken an interest in me: "Everyone seems to have a problem with what I do. They think we are bad people. That's why I enjoy talking to you. I want to make it known that we are okay people, too."

That conversation, and that trip, convinced me of the need to write this book. To do that, I made repeated trips out to Mustang Ranch and Nevada's other brothels over the next four years, spending a total of nearly seven months there. It is not my intent to redeem these women—they don't need my help—but to awaken readers to their humanity and bring this issue out of the realm of caricature and into that of serious debate. That would be more than enough.

2 .. AN INSTITUTION

You could say that I have something of a history with prostitution. That history began in earnest in 1988, when I was a twenty-year-old psychology major. I read an article in *Psychology Today* asserting that juvenile prostitutes were at risk of becoming part of the AIDS epidemic. The article estimated that there were 1.2 million runaway and homeless teens nationwide, some 20,000 to 40,000 in New York City alone, and that between 125,000 and 200,000 each year turned to prostitution to survive on the streets. Selling sex—principally condomless sex—to strangers and abusing illicit drugs significantly increased these kids' risk of HIV infection.

The article mentioned Streetwork, a drop-in center in New York City's Times Square run by a former prostitute whose underfunded agency furnished social services to the runaway, throwaway, and otherwise homeless adolescents who worked the streets of Hell's Kitchen to get by. A refuge from the dangers of the street, the center offered counseling, meals, clothing, showers, and laundry facilities to help the teens regain some of their dignity and self-esteem. Inspired, I managed to get a job there that summer as an outreach worker.

For three months, I watched adolescents supply a staggering demand of adult men seeking out teens for impulsive, reckless sexual recreation—in their cars, in subway and bus stations, in seedy hotels, in alleys, and sometimes right on the street. Except for centers like Streetwork, the only affirmation these kids received came from the men who sought to abuse their bodies. This demand seemed never-ending, despite the well-publicized risks of unprotected sex.

Most of the adolescents had fled troubled homes, neglect, or outright abuse, and they had few resources. Most came to the streets with developmental handicaps and minimal education. The imminent hazards of street prostitution—HIV infection, drug addiction, incarceration, rape, and murder—only isolated these teens further. By the end of my summer, I came to regard the downward spiral of prostitution as inevitable and inexorable.

My experience at Streetwork thus informed many of my initial assumptions about Nevada's brothel prostitution. I couldn't believe a state in America would actually choose to legalize this atrocity. Were Nevadans amoral? What sort of cruel, detached people condoned a profession that brought such pain on its practitioners? While I *had* considered the possibility that legalization might eliminate some of the perils of street prostitution and that Nevadans were actually brave pragmatists, I was skeptical.

I learned quickly that nothing I knew accounted for Nevada's singularity in deciding to license prostitution. Brothel prostitution has been tolerated in the state for over a century; houses of prostitution have operated unobtrusively since the gold- and silver-rush days of the Comstock Lode, between 1859 and 1880. But unlike California, Arizona, and Colorado, which also tolerated brothel prostitution during the mining days, only Nevada would go on doing so. In the northeastern town of Elko, one licensed brothel now known as Mona's has been operating since 1902.

Like a boastful parent, almost every longtime Nevada resident I met regaled me with brothel folklore. As far as I could make out from their tales, prostitutes first arrived in Nevada on the heels of the gold and silver prospectors, to fulfill what was then considered an important social need. At a time when men far outnumbered women on the frontier, prostitutes were welcome new additions. Every gold-rush town had a red-light district, and prostitution became a flourishing industry in mining towns such as Goldfield and Tonopah. At one point, over 50 brothels operated in Virginia City.

Some locals quoted their forefathers to prove the civic-mindedness behind their state's permissive stance on prostitution. I heard James Scrugham, a Nevada governor in the 1920s, quoted more than once: "The camps were not for wives. They just couldn't put up with the roughness. . . . The miners, some coming in from a day in the drifts, some coming from months of prospecting, hands callused, boots worn, having smelled only sagebrush and sweat . . . why, the poor bastards knew the one place they could get a welcome, a smile, a bed with springs, clean sheets, the smell of perfume, was the crib [a string of small shacks where prostitutes would work]."

Several of Nevada's frontier prostitutes have become legends, particularly over the last century. Like Julia Bulette, a well-known prostitute at the time who worked in some of the Comstock's best brothels before she was brutally murdered in 1867 by a customer. It is said that Virginia City's Fire Engine Company No. 1 elected her to be an honorary member, "in return for numerous favors and munificent gifts bestowed by her upon the company."* After her untimely and tragic death, the *Territorial Enterprise* wrote, "Few of her class had more friends." Fire Engine Company No. 1 marched in her funeral procession through the streets of Virginia City. The public execution by hanging (the first for the city) of her alleged killer drew more than four thousand spectators, including Mark Twain, who was touring the country. But according to Nevada State Archivist Guy Rocha, it is twentieth-century writers of Nevada's history who are responsible for creating Bulette's bigger-than-life legend with their romanticized and glamorized writings of her life. Even the Virginia and Truckee railroad line contributed to her mythical status when they named a club car

*Cited in The Mythical West: An Encyclopedia of Legend, Lore, and Popular Culture, edited by Richard W. Slatta, ABC-CLIO, Inc., 2001.

after her in 1947, eighty years after her death, as a publicity gimmick.

As soon as "respectable" women and their families traveled west to join their men, however, lawmakers realized they would need to regulate prostitution if they were to keep it tolerable to their evolving populace. Legislators passed the first law to control prostitution in 1881; it vested county commissions with the power to "license, tax, regulate, prohibit, or suppress all houses of ill-fame." Continuous pressure from community groups led the state legislature to prohibit brothels both on main business thoroughfares and within four hundred yards of schools, and later churches, for the presumed protection of public morality. (Refusing to cede their brothel, legend has it that the people of the old mining town of Searchlight in the 1920s complied with the law by moving the school.)

By the turn of the century, prostitution flourished in Nevada's principal cities, Reno and Las Vegas, though it was limited to specific zones. Block 16, downtown and only a block from the staid First State Bank, became Vegas's designated red-light district, while Reno confined its brothels to a stretch on the east end of town along the Truckee River called the Stockade, or the Riverside restricted district. The Stockade included a dance hall, a restaurant for working girls, and fifty cribs—austere rooms containing a bed, chest of drawers, and a wood-burning stove. These rooms could be rented out twenty-four hours a day in eight-hour shifts for $2.50. Prostitutes were required to register with the police and to visit the city doctor regularly.

Reno's Stockade and Las Vegas's Block 16 prospered until

1942, when a presidential executive order under Franklin D. Roosevelt directed the states to suppress all prostitution near military bases and installations. While soldiers might have had the same "needs" as miners of the Old West, the military feared that sexually transmitted diseases, particularly syphilis, could incapacitate their forces. Nevadans opposed the federal government's intervention but did not want to suffer the economic hardship that would result if their communities were declared off-limits to military personnel. Not until the end of World War II and the lifting of the war emergency in 1948 would regulation of brothel prostitution be returned to local agencies.

At this point, however, authorities in Las Vegas and Reno decided to take a less tolerant position on brothel prostitution. The casino industry was blossoming; in an effort to avoid a federal crackdown on gambling, Vegas and Reno attempted to divorce that business from organized crime and prostitution. When a madam named Mae Cunningham challenged the closure of her Reno brothel in 1949, a judge ruled that county commissioners and district attorneys had the authority to abate brothels as "public nuisances," even though Nevada had no statute explicitly barring prostitution.

Panicked that the outcome of the Cunningham case endangered all of Nevada's brothels, rural libertarian lawmakers hurriedly signed a bill that explicitly gave counties the "local option" to legalize brothels. But powerful prodding from increasingly influential casino owners forced the governor, Vail Pitman, to veto this bill. He defended his actions by saying that legalization would result in "sensational and sordid publicity" throughout America. Using the Cunningham case as precedent, brothels that had opened after World War II in and around Reno (e.g., Mae Cunningham's) and Las Vegas (e.g., Roxie's) were closed as public nuisances.

Brothel prostitution would change forever in 1955 with the appearance of Joe Conforte, the future owner of the Mustang Ranch and the man who would ultimately be responsible for legalizing brothel prostitution. A Sicilian immigrant with the tenacity of a bulldog and the narcissism of Napoleon, Conforte had been a cabdriver and sex broker from Oakland who came to Nevada intent on exploiting the state's spotty and arbitrarily enforced prostitution laws. When he met resistance trying to establish a house in Reno, he settled upon a patch of alfalfa pasture in Storey County, just outside Washoe County. Here, in Wadsworth, he built the Triangle River Ranch. Within five months, he had partnered with his future wife, Sally Burgess, who had operated a house in Fallon, Nevada, and had purchased three more brothels.

Conforte, who would later attribute his prosperity to the "Three B's"—brains, breaks, and balls—wasn't one to keep his success quiet. Well aware of Washoe County's antibrothel position, Conforte regularly enjoyed strutting through Reno, sporting expensive suits, a full-length fur coat, $18 Cuban cigars, and a $4,000 hair transplant, with several prostitutes draped on each arm. It wasn't unusual for Joe to pass out crisp $100 bills and brothel passes to card dealers and busboys. Feeling that Conforte was making a mockery of law and decency, Washoe County district attorney William Raggio (who served from 1958 to 1970 as D.A. and today is the Nevada State Senate majority leader) became incensed.

In his first act of aggression—many were to follow, in a long-ensuing feud between the two men—Raggio charged Conforte with vagrancy whenever he came into Reno. Raggio also got word to Reno's main gambling houses and restaurants that Conforte should not be served. In retaliation, Conforte cooked up an elaborate plot to catch Raggio buying a seventeen-year-old girl (a minor) alcoholic drinks and having sex with her. Conforte threatened to make this scandal public if Raggio failed to back off on the vagrancy charges. Unbeknownst to Conforte, however, Raggio taped this incriminatory conversation, including Conforte's bribe, resulting in Conforte's arrest for attempted extortion of a public official; he appealed the conviction for many years before he finally had to serve time. (To this day, Raggio publicly denies seducing the young girl.)

Raggio still wasn't satisfied. He managed to persuade Storey County authorities to use the precedent set by the Cunningham case to close Conforte's Wadsworth brothel on the grounds that it was a public nuisance. Not convinced that this alone would stop Conforte, Raggio also persuaded the Storey County district attorney and Sparks Fire Department chief to descend upon the Wadsworth pasture with him one night with media in tow, and torched it. Raggio claimed he had a right to burn down the brothel because of its status as a public nuisance, even though the brothel was located outside of his jurisdiction. Sally Conforte, however, sued him for damages, charging him with illegal burning. The case was eventually settled. After the fire, Conforte consolidated his business into a trailer that he situated at the juncture of Washoe, Storey, and Lyon counties. Whenever authorities in one county threatened to close him down, he moved the trailer across county lines.

While Conforte was away in prison on the extortion conviction, a competitor named Richard Bennet appeared on the Storey County scene. Bennet persuaded the county commissioners to let him open a brothel, Mustang Bridge Ranch; he picked a little-noticed spot in Storey County that was within twelve miles of Reno—twenty-seven miles closer than Wadsworth—on a ranch owned by two brothers, Jim and Joe Peri. Bennet convinced the Peris to rent him the land, and, like Conforte, bought four double-wide trailers, linking them into a compound. When Conforte emerged from prison almost three years later, more ambitious and driven than ever, he was enraged by his competitor's good fortune, enjoyed at his expense. In what Conforte called his "comeback" phase, involving a series of dubious events about which locals are unclear, including several mysterious fires and the detonation of the suspension bridge over the Truckee River near Bennet's Mustang Bridge Ranch, Conforte managed to drive out his competition. In 1967, rumor has it, Bennet "voluntarily" sold his brothel to Conforte for an undisclosed sum.

With Mustang Bridge Ranch now his, Conforte allegedly schemed to regain control of the county. To get more sympathetic politicians elected into county offices, Conforte enlarged a nearby settlement called Lockwood by adding trailers and offering tenants cheap rents in implicit exchange for voting in local elections as he suggested. In this way, and by making regular contributions to politicians, Conforte became a major political influence in the county.

It was in this context that, in 1970, Conforte suggested the county pass the nation's first brothel-licensing ordinance. Not surprisingly, he met little resistance. To assist officials in defending their legislation, Conforte suggested that the licensing fee be so high that it would be impractical fiscally not to legalize prostitution. He recommended a fee of $18,000 per year, later raised to $25,000. (As of 2000, the fee is set at $100,000.) As Conforte expected, Storey County officials jumped at his proposal; brothel prostitution in the county became legal on January 1, 1971. A Nevada Supreme Court decision upheld Storey County's right to legalize prostitution; simultaneously, permissiveness was permeating the culture. Reno officials finally let up on Conforte. (The feud between Raggio and Conforte continued for some time, however. As a state senator, Raggio tried unsuccessfully to ban brothels within fifty miles of major cities, a proposal that would have closed only Conforte's brothel.)

Meanwhile, Storey County's new ordinance sent the rest of the state into a tizzy. When Las Vegas hotel and casino operators and convention bureau officials caught wind that Conforte—now feeling all-powerful—wanted to open a brothel at the edge of their city, they lobbied state lawmakers to pass emergency legislation making brothel prostitution illegal in counties with more than 200,000 people. At that time, in

1971, this population threshold applied only to Las Vegas's Clark County. (Meant to apply exclusively to Clark County—without being considered "selective legislation"—this law is amended and the population limit increased routinely whenever other counties, namely Washoe, begin creeping up in size approaching this maximum; today the population threshold is prescribed at 400,000.) In contrast, commissioners in Nevada's rural counties were thrilled by the prospect of licensing their brothels—Nevada had between thirty and forty houses as of 1969—and generating a new source of county revenue. In 1972, county commissioners in Lyon County licensed their three existing brothels. Between 1973 and 1978, three other counties—Churchill, Mineral, and Nye—legalized brothel prostitution in restricted areas following favorable public referendum votes.

As of early 2000, there were twenty-six brothels in Nevada, scattered throughout ten of the state's seventeen counties. (Sixteen counties plus Carson City, considered the Capital District, which enjoys all the benefits of a county, such as having its own courthouse and police and fire departments.) Three of the ten—Elko, Humboldt, and White Pine—prohibit brothel prostitution in unincorporated areas, but do allow it by municipal option in the cities of Elko, Wells, Carlin, Ely, and Winnemucca. Each county has devised its own brothel ordinance, from Lyon County's exhaustive forty-eight-page document to Esmeralda County's more terse seven-page code. Brothel licensing fees vary, with Storey County's being the highest ($25,000 per quarter) and Lander County's the lowest ($50 per quarter). Brothel regulations differ on details such as the size, content, and placement of exterior signs, and the wattage of red exterior lighting permitted on brothel premises. Only five counties have opted to outlaw brothels, including those that contain Reno, Lake Tahoe, and Carson City. (Two counties—Eureka and Pershing—have yet to address the matter formally.)

But times and county demographics are changing. A recent editorial in the *Reno Gazette-Journal* declared that the legal brothels "stamp Nevada as a hick state mired in an outmoded and unsavory past." Nevada is currently undergoing one of the fastest rates of growth in the nation, with a population increase of 44 percent between 1990 and 1997. Brothel owners and county officials contend that the recent influx of transplants who don't understand or appreciate Nevada's peculiar history and libertarian ideals threaten the survival of this century-old state institution. Consequently, they argue, regulation of the industry is ever more important to keep brothel prostitution tolerable to Nevada's expanding population.

NEW PROSTITUTES GOT a taste of these regulations as soon as they applied to a brothel for employment. When a woman named Eva arrived at Mustang Ranch looking for a job, I saw firsthand just how formalized, not to say bureaucratized, was the process of becoming a licensed brothel prostitute.

Eva pulled up in front of Mustang #2 in her '84 Chevy one afternoon around two o'clock. She had followed the instructions she had been given on the telephone: to ring the doorbell on the electric fence twice, not once, so the working girls would know it wasn't a customer. They didn't want to line up for nothing. When Irene, the manager, greeted her at the front door, Eva explained that she had called about a position as a working girl. Irene chuckled warmheartedly and said she got calls all day long from women looking for jobs as prostitutes. By noon on this particular day, six women had already called. Mustang Ranch received nearly a dozen telephone inquiries a day. It didn't seem to matter much that the brothels weren't permitted by law to advertise for prostitutes.

With fifty-four bedrooms in #1 and thirty-eight in #2, Mustang could hire a maximum of ninety-two women but usually chose to cap the number of prostitutes at seventy-five. The brothel usually approached capacity over the weekend and then thinned out at the start of the week. (Mustang's scheduling practices have evolved over the years and the brothel no longer requires women to work three weeks on, one week off; some women, especially those who live nearby, work a four- to five-day week, leaving Sunday or Monday and returning on Wednesday or Thursday.) In a year's time, about 515 prostitutes came through Mustang Ranch. Since hiring over the telephone was a potential violation of both interstate commerce and pimping and pandering laws (under the Mann Act of 1910), brothels required in-person interviews.

A woman in her early twenties, Eva physically reminded me of the model Kate Moss, with her serene, creamy face, delicate, waiflike facial features, and petite, nubile body. She parted her fine, dishwater-blond hair in the middle and let it fall naturally below her shoulders. Eva was beautiful in the most natural of ways, with a preference for patchouli oil over department store fragrances and no interest in makeup. She was a sure hire, I thought, and I expected Irene to offer her a position immediately. I was surprised to hear her explain that Eva would need to spend the next two days meeting a number of requirements before she could be hired as a licensed prostitute.

Irene led Eva back to her office and invited her to sit down on one of the red folding chairs cluttering the room. How had Eva heard about Mustang Ranch? Irene asked. Eva took a deep breath before explaining that she'd been working as a cashier in a gentleman's club in Sacramento, struggling to pay off a credit card debt of over $30,000. Some of the dancers had suggested she try prostitution, but Eva had been too scared. She was afraid of getting arrested or being killed by a deranged customer. One of the women told her about Nevada's legal brothels. Irene quizzed Eva some more about her background, asking about her previous work experience and home life. Somewhat defensive, Eva made a point of telling Irene that she came from a stable middle-class home with a functional family and married parents.

After a few minutes, Irene shifted gears and began describing the conditions under which Eva would be working. Specifically, all working girls were restricted to the immediate brothel confines (save for outdates, or paid excursions with clients) for the duration of their stay, which ranged from days to weeks depending upon their financial goals. Even though Eva had just rented an apartment in nearby Reno, she couldn't go home after her shift. The rationale was simple: owners worried about the women "freelancing," turning tricks on the outside.

I would later discover that police and brothel owners had worked in collusion for many years to enforce unofficial codes of conduct that segregated prostitutes from the communities in which they worked, although no law quarantining brothel prostitutes was actually on the books. For example, on the pretext of protecting public decency, the town of Winnemucca in Humboldt County prohibited brothel prostitutes from frequenting town bars, casinos, or residential areas, associating with local men outside of work, being on the downtown streets after five P.M., or having any family members residing in town. Violation of any one of these rules could result in confiscation of a woman's brothel work card and her expulsion from town. (Because brothel work cards and licenses were considered "privileged" licenses, they could be revoked for any reason.)

Finally, in 1984, Reno attorney Richard Hager filed a federal lawsuit against Winnemucca, contending the rules violated the constitutional rights of prostitutes who had been fired for breaking them. "Is it acceptable or tolerable for a community to license commercial sex and yet discriminate against the women who provide it?" wrote Ellen Pillard, a professor at the University of Nevada–Reno and occasional brothel critic, in an article entitled "Legal Prostitution: Is It Just?" "That would be like licensing gambling, but prohibiting 21 dealers from living in the community." Following the filing of the women's lawsuit, Winnemucca and several other towns that had similar regulations (e.g., Ely, Elko, Wells, Lovelock, and Battle Mountain) discarded their unlawful codes of conduct, although to this day brothel management and law enforcement still try to limit prostitutes' contact with local communities. Mustang Ranch, for example, required a runner, or escort, to accompany prostitutes on errands to town at the women's own expense—$5–$10 per errand or stop.

Women's activities were strictly controlled within the brothel gates as well. Each bedroom was equipped with a hidden intercom system that cashiers used to eavesdrop on women's negotiations to assure they didn't steal money from the house or trade sex for drugs. Women were told to turn off their radios, televisions, and ceiling fans when discussing money with customers so as not to muffle the sound of their negotiations. Despite this deterrent to theft, stealing was ubiquitous. Out of intercom range in the hallways, prostitutes whispered to customers their plans to quote aloud a reduced price if the man would agree to silently hand over an additional sum of money. With multiple prostitutes negotiating simultaneously, women also gambled that the cashier wasn't listening, and turned in less money than was actually paid. To combat theft and drug use, management conducted unannounced room searches, led by floor maids who had been brothel prostitutes and knew all the places a woman might hide money or drugs: in bars of soap, hair spray cans, mattresses, and air vents.

After Irene spelled out the restrictions on Eva's movement, she explained that Mustang Ranch hired prostitutes as independent contractors, which meant the brothel wasn't responsible for withholding taxes from the women's earnings. It would be Eva's responsibility to submit a copy of the Form 1099 filed on her behalf by Mustang with her taxes. (In actuality, however, there has never been close to 100 percent compliance by either prostitutes or owners in filing 1099s.) In return, as an independent contractor, she could set her own work schedule and negotiate her own prices with customers. Eva would be expected to split her gross earnings 50–50 with the brothel. In addition, she would be docked $31 daily: $10 to cover room and board and $21 to tip seven brothel employees $3 apiece: the manager, the cook, the floor maids, a laundry maid, and two cashiers. In exchange, Eva would receive three warm meals a day, with twenty-four-hour access to additional snacks, and be assigned a bedroom in which to work and live for the duration of her stay, with an adjoining bathroom shared with her next-door neighbor.

As I listened to Irene explain the terms to Eva, I reflected on their inequity. Owners got away with not paying employee-related federal and local taxes or social security, and making the women tip brothel staff kept other labor costs down. At the same time, as independent contractors, women lost out on employee benefits ranging from health insurance and sick leave to disability insurance and workers' compensation. (In all fairness, Nevada state authorities, too, have been reluctant to offer legal prostitutes any form of benefit package for fear of the potential expense.)

I wondered if these women were really afforded the rights due independent contractors. Soon enough, Eva would learn that working girls were obliged to give a share of their earnings to cabdrivers because of a financial arrangement worked out with brothel owners many years ago. Because state law prohibited brothels from advertising, even from publishing their addresses or telephone numbers, the brothels depended upon cabbies to inform passengers of their whereabouts. In return, the drivers got 20 percent of what their passengers spent at the brothel; 10 percent came out of the prostitute's cut and 10 percent out of the brothel's. To guarantee their kickback, most drivers accompanied their passengers into the brothel and waited in the kitchen until their fare negotiated a party, at which point cabbies would be informed of their portion, available for pickup within twenty-four hours.

Prostitutes were also expected to split their tips from customers with the house, even though a tip reflected the quality of service that each woman personally rendered. Moreover, all brothels had house minimums, ranging from $50 to $150. When a woman refused a customer willing to pay the house minimum, management expected a reasonable excuse (e.g., that he refused to wear a condom). While Eva would negotiate her own deals and could raise her prices to deter unappealing customers, management would raise its eyebrows if she did this too often.

The brothel was less concerned with racism, however. Women were always permitted to opt out of servicing black customers. Discrimination against black clients was not new to Nevada's brothels. For many years, none of the brothels even admitted black men. Then, in 1967, at the suggestion of one of Joe Conforte's floor maids, a black woman named Alberta (affectionately nicknamed Miss Bertie by the working girls), Conforte constructed a parlor to accommodate black clients, segregated in classic Jim Crow fashion. Inside the front gate, a separate entranceway led to this smaller, adjoining parlor; jukebox music from the main parlor was piped in. With the arrival of a black patron, willing women went over to the second parlor to line up while their unwilling peers remained in the main parlor. It wasn't unusual for a group of black men to confront a lineup comprised of one lone woman. Only when Conforte built the current Mustang #1 facility, a permanent structure more upscale than the hodgepodge of double-wide trailers hooked together, would blacks share the main parlor with other races.

Referred to as Parlor Two guests to this day, black customers are still treated differently. Whenever a black man rang Mustang's doorbell, the cashier or security guard monitoring the front gate sounded a distinct, shrill in-house buzzer twice, summoning only those women willing to party with a black man to line up. Rung once, the buzzer indicated the arrival of a nonblack customer by cab; three rings indicated the arrival of a black man by cab. Women who won't entertain black customers have to quit the parlor until after the black man views his lineup.

While most of the women at Mustang Ranch lined up for black customers, about one-fourth wouldn't. Most of these women told me that their men at home had asked them not to accept black clients. Curiously, most of those men were themselves black. Rather than deep-seated hatred of their own race, this prejudice seemed to reflect fear of losing their women to another black man. For women without the excuse of a man at home, racism was the only explanation for rejection. Too willingly, brothel management refused to challenge these prostitutes. "We get a lot of girls from the South," said Irene. "You can't force a girl from Texas or the South to take someone to her bedroom who her parents and grandparents have been racist against for years." Then, apparently unaware of any irony, she added, "That would be like slavery."

After Irene finished explaining how prostitutes' earnings were split with the house, she asked Eva whether she had any questions. Eva said she had none. Irene asked one last question: How did Eva think she would be able to handle screwing men for money if she had never done it before? Irene's voice was detached, and her face was a blank mask. Later, she told me that she worked hard not to become emotionally invested in any of the girls until they were officially hired. Moreover, she was proud of how discerning she was. "I won't just hire any girl that walks in the door. Some managers do. An awful lot of managers see each girl as an extra three-dollar tip a day in their pocket. With five extra girls, you've almost got your mortgage payment."

Among the criteria most important to Irene was the applicant's response to that last question. "I always ask new turn-outs if they've thought about what they'll have to do as a prostitute," she said. "Most tell me they've seen *Pretty Woman* or that they like sex. I say, 'Wait a minute. This job is tough. Some of these guys are fat, some are ugly, and some have B.O. These guys are going to tell you to spread your legs or to give them a blow job. Have you thought about that?' From the look on their faces, I can see most of them haven't." Eva's candid answer—that she was scared but hoped as a professional she would learn to block out any negative thoughts—was satisfactory; afterward, Irene announced she had passed the first test on the way to being hired.

If Eva met the remaining requirements, Irene wanted to hire her as a day girl, to work the shift from eleven A.M. to eleven P.M. According to Irene, day and night girls needed different personalities. Those who did well as day girls were more reserved and conventional, whereas night girls needed to be able to hustle and party. Irene preferred to start all new turn-outs as day girls. Mustang was open twenty-four hours a day, seven days a week, and women worked twelve-hour shifts (fourteen hours on Fridays and Saturdays): early (eleven A.M.– eleven P.M.) middle (three P.M.–three A.M.), or late (eleven P.M.– eleven A.M.). I discovered later that brothels in more rural, outlying areas, with less traffic, had all their prostitutes work the same shift—from noon or one to two or three A.M., at which point lineups were suspended and the prostitutes were allowed to go to bed. Those who'd done the least business were given the choice of being "early up" girls, servicing customers who came in between four A.M. and one P.M. A few brothels used photo albums to introduce available women rather than to rouse them from their sleep.

Irene was respectful throughout the interview, but I heard horror stories from some of the prostitutes about other managers and owners with unorthodox interview practices. A few required women to disrobe to examine their bodies, checking for track marks as well as for the quality of their physique.

When Eva, Irene, and I finally emerged from Irene's office after the thirty-minute interview, the UPS man was delivering a shipment of five thousand condoms ordered forty-eight hours earlier, direct from the manufacturer. This reminded Irene of something that had almost slipped her mind. "Eva, you know you have to use condoms with all your customers?" she said sternly. Since 1988, the Bureau of Disease Control and Intervention Services for the Nevada State Health Division has required brothel patrons to use latex condoms for all sexual activity with brothel prostitutes. Eva already knew this, having seen the sign on the front gate. Houses of prostitution were required to post a public health notice stating that although Nevada state law required that every brothel prostitute be tested regularly and that customers wear condoms, this did not guarantee freedom from STDs. As he stood there waiting for Irene to sign the receipt, the UPS man couldn't help interjecting, "And the condom companies love you for it."

I tagged along as another prostitute showed Eva down Hallway D to a vacant room. Like mine, it was about twelve feet by ten feet, painted dusty pink, with pink-champagne wall-to-wall carpeting. The walls were bare, save for a litter of pushpins and pieces of Scotch tape left by the previous tenant. White bedding covered the full-size mattress situated on a wooden box frame. The only other piece of furniture was a dresser made from particleboard, on top of which sat a black plastic ashtray. A crooked vertical blind covered the lone window, which looked out onto the desert landscape. The other prostitute advised Eva to fix up her room a bit, using pillows, artificial plants, posters, pictures, and mirrors. Plain and bare, the empty room looked more like a cell than a boudoir. Indeed, it was difficult to imagine a customer finding this room erotic. Eva was also told she should store her valuables in the closet and padlock the door.

Eva hadn't brought much with her. She had hoped to go home before starting work. Women with more experience generally came to their interviews loaded down with suitcases and garbage bags filled with personal belongings. Irene suggested that Eva begin the time-consuming process of getting licensed, and then the brothel runner could drive her home to collect some of her possessions. Irene also gave her a list of essentials: water-based lubricant; condoms; Betadine and baby wipes to clean the customers; mouthwash; vitamin E capsules to insert in her vagina to soothe the irritation of frequent intercourse; Mentholatum to spread on tampons, also to help relieve vaginal soreness; cosmetic sponges for use during menstruation to absorb heavy flow; a bathrobe; and a disinfectant to wipe down the toilet seat and bidet after each client.

Over the next two days, Eva busied herself getting licensed, a process involving several steps. First, the brothel runner drove Eva to the brothel physician's office, where she was tested for STDs, including HIV, to obtain a valid health certificate. Since 1986, the state legislature had required that all brothel prostitutes be tested for HIV as a condition of employment; once employed, they were tested monthly. In 1987, the legislature further decided that owners could be held liable for damages caused to any patron exposed to HIV as a result of the continued employment of an HIV-positive prostitute. Long before the industry was legalized, however, brothel prostitutes were getting tested regularly for STDs. Back in 1937, Nevada inaugurated an aggressive venereal disease prevention program that required prostitutes to have weekly medical exams for gonorrhea and monthly blood tests for syphilis. In 1992, counties added chlamydia to the weekly test.

Women seeking employment were not allowed to work until all tests came back negative. The labs that performed the tests were to call or fax all positive results to the STD/HIV/TB program of the state's Bureau of Disease Control and Intervention Services as well as to brothel medical providers. If a woman tested positive for an STD other than HIV, the medical provider notified the brothel as well as the county sheriff, who pulled the prostitute's work card until she underwent a course of treatment. In some counties, working girls were obligated to use certain medical providers, selected by either the brothels or county commissioners, whereas other counties allowed prostitutes to see the physician of their choice. Health care costs could be sizable: $50 for each weekly exam and $85 for the monthly exam that included HIV and syphilis testing.

Customers weren't obligated to be tested for anything. (Practically speaking, testing clients would be close to impossible.) But brothel prostitutes had long been inspecting men's genitals before sex to screen out customers with STDs. Once hired, Eva would be paired with a more senior working girl who would teach her how to examine a customer's penis for visible signs of disease. In no time, she would become an adept clinician, proficient in looking for signs of gonorrhea ("yellow-white discharge"), chlamydia ("watery white drip"), warts (small, painless bumps), herpes (small blisters), and crabs (pinhead-sized insect parasites). When a prostitute found a suspicious lesion, she called in another working girl, a floor maid, or a manager for a "d/c," or double check. If her suspicions were confirmed, the woman was supposed to give the customer a pamphlet from the Bureau of Disease Control and Intervention Services that explained he might have an STD and advised him to seek medical care. For a fee of $60, women could treat men for crabs on the spot. Men who passed inspection had their genitals cleansed thoroughly by the prostitute, on either the bidet or a "peter pan," a small plastic dishwater pan, using soap or Betadine as a disinfectant.

At the conclusion of Eva's medical exam, with verification of her doctor's visit in hand, she and the runner headed to the sheriff substation two miles from Mustang Ranch in the Lockwood Mobile Home Park, where she registered for a work card.

Manning the substation for the Storey County Sheriff's Department was Sergeant Bill Petty, a fifty-nine-year-old former Navy man with a military-style flattop. Any felony conviction, he explained, would bar a woman from becoming licensed, as would a conviction related to fraud, embezzlement, misappropriation of funds, or larceny; unlawful possession or distribution of narcotics; unlawful use of a pistol or other dangerous weapon; unlawful entry of a building; buying or receiving stolen property; or any sexual offense or crime involving "moral turpitude." Other counties had similar ordinances. In 1996, the city of Winnemucca became the first to issue brothel work cards to women previously convicted of misdemeanor offenses such as shoplifting.

After Petty finished his introduction—it was more for my

benefit, I think, than Eva's—he turned to Eva and asked if she had already been to the doctor. Silently, she handed him the certificate that verified she had been tested earlier in the day for gonorrhea, chlamydia, syphilis, and HIV, with results pending. Petty pulled out an application form that asked for the name she was given at birth; all subsequent aliases and assumed names; her birth date; her address; a physical description (race, height, weight, hair and eye colors, and "marks, scars, tattoos"); her three-year employment record; and an explanation of any previous arrests. (Brothel owners had to complete a similar application to obtain a brothel license.) She would also have to sign a waiver to authorize both the release of subsequent medical information and an investigation into her criminal history.

As Eva wrote, Petty squinted, studying her.

"How old *are* you, miss?" he asked.

Startled, Eva looked up at Petty. Up until now, she had tried to avoid eye contact with him. She felt self-conscious and nervous at revealing to a law enforcement agent her intention of becoming a prostitute. But he expected a response, and she didn't want to mess things up. She said she was twenty-one. Petty asked to see some photo identification and her Social Security card while she finished up the application.

Petty was cautious because of a recent scandal in which he'd been involved, having to do with the licensing of underage girls. He had mistakenly approved the fake identification of two minors seeking employment at Storey County's third brothel, Old Bridge Ranch. However, Petty claimed, underage prostitutes were rare in his county. Police from Oregon, where the two minors came from, were less certain; they claimed that underage girls secured work as prostitutes in Nevada brothels using fake identification far more often than either the brothels or law enforcement liked to admit. Joe Conforte's nephew, David Burgess, who owned the Old Bridge Ranch, defended the system to the media, asserting that his managers did everything they could to avoid hiring underage girls, but "If they've got the proper ID, there's no way we can tell." Remorseful about the incidents, Petty went out of his way to attest that he had always been very conscientious about verifying women's identification and age. Since the brouhaha he had tried to intensify his scrutiny.

Storey and Lyon counties were the only counties in Nevada to grant brothel work cards to eighteen-year-olds. Elsewhere in the state, the minimum age was twenty-one. There was no upper age limit, although I met few working girls beyond their mid-forties. The exception was Dinah, Mustang Ranch's oldest prostitute at sixty-three. Dinah had turned her first trick at fifty-one. "My first day, I lied when the manager asked me about previous work experience," she told me one day at Mustang #1. "Of course I had never done it before. But I was a much older lady—almost fifty-two years old." With a touch of a Southern drawl, she explained her atypical entry into the profession: "I was a virgin until I got married. My husband was an Ivy League graduate—stable, reliable, a provider. I had it all. But we weren't compatible sexually. He was too big, and I didn't get excited the way I should have. When it hurt, I went to doctors, who told me it was my fault; I wasn't making enough lubrication. I hated to go to bed because he wanted sex. I would stay up all night, washing, cleaning, and ironing, so I didn't have to go upstairs. I don't blame him for getting another woman."

After her divorce, Dinah began dating, and found she could enjoy sex after all. However, her fresh independence brought new financial struggles—she was a single mom striving to get two sons through school—until a colleague told her about Nevada's brothels. "You give it away, don't you?" said her friend, alluding to Dinah's promiscuity. Determined to provide for her kids, she decided to give prostitution a try. She astonished herself when she earned $4,300 in her first fourteen days at the brothel. Since then, she had come to Nevada regularly for three-week stints, telling her family she was away on business.

Although she was always cordial, Dinah kept mainly to herself at Mustang. Typically, she sat alone at one end of the bar throughout most of her shift. In spite of her aloofness, Dinah kept an eye on the Mustang scene and always had gossip to dish, of which I often became the recipient. For Dinah, the trip to the sheriff's substation to get licensed had been more terrifying than turning her first trick. Already apprehensive about her new venture, Dinah said that although the sheriff was perfectly professional, facing him was terrible. "I turned out at the Sagebrush Ranch in Lyon County. I'll never forget my first visit to the sheriff's office to register. The application asked which position I was applying for. I stared at the two boxes—one that said 'Maid' and the other 'Prostitute'—for the longest time. It was like I couldn't bring myself to check off 'Prostitute.' I nearly died before I managed to mark off the right box." Unlike Lyon County, Storey County used a euphemism to lessen women's embarrassment: Petty told Eva to write "Entertainer" as her professional title.

Once Petty was satisfied with Eva's application, he photocopied her two pieces of identification and accepted her $50 cash to cover the licensing fee, which would be submitted with her application to Storey County officials in Virginia City. The final steps of the licensing process involved taking two Polaroid photographs—one for her file and another for her work card—and then fingerprinting her. The print, of her right index finger, would be used in Virginia City to confirm her identification and search for outstanding warrants. Petty said that few applicants actually had any history of previous altercations with the law, save for occasional speeding tickets, but a few days later, he was to handcuff a new blond turn-out and escort her dramatically out of Mustang. She had four warrants for her arrest.

After county officials processed Eva's application, Petty would deliver to Mustang Ranch her laminated lime-green work card, her official documentation authorizing her to prostitute in the named brothel. Prostitutes could only be approved to work at one licensed operation at a time; if Eva chose to change brothels, she would need to reapply and pay another $50 licensing fee. (Not infrequently, women moved from brothel to brothel as the seasons changed and business fluctuated.) Brothel management retained each woman's work card, in preparation for the next impromptu inspection by the sheriff. Meanwhile, back at the Ranch, Eva would need to wait a minimum of twenty-four hours to "clear," or receive the results of her STD tests. Once the tests came back negative, she would be a licensed prostitute.

I was surprised that licensing was such a rigorous process, but that was precisely the idea behind legalization: to impose a number of conditions upon an otherwise unruly enterprise as a means of control. "Within our society, we have no choice as to whether or not we want this fact of life called prostitution," Joe Conforte was fond of telling his critics. "You are not going to eliminate prostitution. Our only real choice in the matter is how we choose to deal with it: control or uncontrol. As long as the business is here, as long as we can't eliminate it, why not organize it?"

Advocates of legalized prostitution, like Conforte and George, were quick to point out that criminalization of prostitution, the policy implemented elsewhere in America, had utterly failed to eradicate the sale of sex. It had succeeded, however, in driving the industry underground, forcing prostitutes to operate on the sly with little recourse against abuse or injury. Criminalization also unjustly targeted prostitutes. Almost always it was prostitutes who were arrested and jailed, not the men who exploited or abused them. (For example, in New York State in 1993, 83 percent of prostitution-related arrests were for soliciting, 11 percent for patronizing a prostitute, and 6 percent for pimping or promoting prostitution.)

But critics argued that regulated, controlled prostitution was merely a wolf in sheep's clothing, that it sanctioned pimping by brothel owners and governments. I had to wonder if there wasn't some truth to that. I had already heard about a few brothel owners who were notorious for exploiting their licensed prostitutes. For example, the owner of a brothel in southern Nevada allegedly confiscated women's personal supplies (condoms, lubricants, nylons) and required them to repurchase everything directly from the brothel at inflated prices, like sharecroppers or miners buying from the company store. And "his" working girls had to buy their meals à la carte from the brothel kitchen, where slabs of tomato cost $2, a box of frozen vegetables $5, and a hamburger $7 (in contrast to Mustang Ranch's flat $10 a day for all you could eat). "The owner took advantage of us, took advantage of the fact we were confined to his brothel," one prostitute divulged to me. "Nothing was free. Everything was overpriced. You couldn't split anything with anybody."

Opponents of the brothels often preferred the abolition of all criminal laws regarding prostitution between consenting adults, including voluntary contractual relationships between prostitutes and their "managers" or pimps. (The mainstream feminist view of prostitution has evolved over time; once most feminists maintained that prostitution was exploitative of women, period, but now a movement has emerged that holds that it's all right for women to do what they want to do.) Decriminalization would also mean the abolition of any statutory regulation of prostitutes, including the requirement of medical examinations and STD workups.

While decriminalization appealed more and more to me as I heard stories about exploitative brothel owners, I was troubled by the idea of eliminating all testing. Mandatory testing violated my sense of a patient's right to privacy, but didn't the public have a right to be protected from potentially transmissible diseases if prostitution was to be legalized? And yet why should a prostitute be singled out among all the other service professionals in contact with the public? Surgeons and dentists, for example, weren't routinely screened for HIV and hepatitis.

For some time, I debated inwardly the question of which model of prostitution seemed most palatable. I still had a lot to learn, especially about what drove women into this profession in the first place.

3 .. BREADWINNERS

Most of the women seemed reluctant to discuss how they got into the business, so I was caught off guard when Donna opened up to me one night at Mustang #1. Donna was a young redhead with a shy smile and thick bangs cut blunt across her forehead, like a toddler's first haircut; I had first noticed her showing her colleagues a book of sexual cartoons. She had put the book together herself, clipping cartoons from magazines like *Playboy*, to entertain her clients while they waited for her to return from booking money with the cashier. It cut down on the number of customers who snooped through her room and stole mementos like underwear and bras, she said.

Donna saw me watching her and invited me over to look at her book. Her customers' favorite, she said, was a cartoon that showed a prostitute being called to the rescue of a man found unconscious on a beach with an erect penis. She watched my face for a reaction. I smiled cautiously, unable to read her own attitude toward the cartoon and not wanting to offend. I must not have, because from that moment on, she and I exchanged pleasantries whenever I visited Mustang #1.

Donna and I frequently ate dinner at the same time, and the night she confided in me, she and I were sitting alone in Mustang's kitchen. Over lasagna and garlic bread, we bantered about the weather, nearby Reno, the casinos. Then, apropos of nothing, she mentioned that her husband couldn't get a job, "because it's hard for someone his age." He was forty-two years old, she said, playing nervously with her wedding band. I wondered where the conversation was headed.

Donna went on to confess, almost apologetically, that she'd never planned to become a prostitute. "One day he came into the kitchen where I was preparing dinner," she said softly. "He said he thought I should start working to support our family. We had all this debt, plus house payments."

At twenty-three, Donna had a five-year-old boy and a three-year-old girl. Aside from baby-sitting as a teenager, the only job she had ever held was as a receptionist in a Reno insurance agency.

"But then he told me he wanted me to work at Mustang Ranch," she said. "He knew several guys whose girlfriends worked there from time to time and earned good money. Of course, I knew what Mustang Ranch was—I've lived in this area my whole life." She couldn't conceal a fleeting grimace.

She said she cried for a week and asked her husband over

and over whether he really wanted her to become a prostitute. He explained the moral and ethical issues as he saw them: he knew she loved him, and he believed that she wouldn't be attracted to the clientele, so it was fine with him. Tearfully, she said she would do whatever he wanted. "Deep down, I didn't think he'd really make me go through with it." She let out a disheartened sigh before recovering her shy smile.

When I met her, Donna had been working at Mustang for one and a half years. She lived at the brothel for a couple of weeks at a time, always returning home with a good deal of money in her purse. Cash was no longer a problem for her family. To go home to her kids and husband, she needed to earn at least $4,000, to cover the monthly bills. Her husband had been incrementally increasing her quota by a couple of hundred dollars over the past several months. I would come to see this vicious cycle frequently, of prostitutes increasing their cost of living with every dollar earned. Consequently, women who had planned to prostitute only briefly found themselves trapped in the business even though they had surpassed their original financial goals.

Until then, out of deference to the women, I had been careful not to pry or try to get too personal. So I was surprised when of her own volition Donna felt compelled to answer the question that was most on my mind: How did you get here? Judging from the questions asked prostitute guests on talk show programs and of me by family members, it was also the question that most preoccupied mainstream America. It was a variant of the "What's a nice girl like you doing in a place like

this?" cliché, asked of any woman who resists the social restrictions that govern most of us and who is involved in types
of behavior we normally classify as "taboo." It's as if knowing
the answer, we can reassure ourselves that we'll never walk in
their shoes.

Prostitutes have been cast as victimizers and victims, as
dead to the pleasure of sex and as too alive to it. Whatever else,
they have always been Other, sufficiently unlike the rest of us
as to evoke sympathy, not empathy. Usually with the best of
intentions, psychologists pathologize prostitutes by suggesting
sweeping causative associations between prostitution and dis-
advantaged situations, physical limitations (e.g., substance
abuse), and previous traumatic experiences, especially sexual
abuse. And knee-jerk moralists speak of prostitutes as flawed
characters lacking in values.

But no easy formula fit the women I met in Nevada's
brothels. Several were black and Latino; a few were Asian and
Native American; fully two-thirds of Mustang's prostitutes
were white. Almost nine out of ten had either graduated from
high school or earned their general equivalency diplomas. While
some of the prostitutes I met came from lower-income families, many grew up well-to-do. Some of the women came from
broken homes with absent fathers, and some had mothers who
had prostituted themselves, but many grew up in intact, functional two-parent households. Although some women admitted to drug and alcohol misuse, the brothel seemed to weed
out women with profound addictions. Fewer than half of the
women spoke to me of childhood sexual abuse, a prevalence

not all that much higher than national estimates that at least 20 percent of American women have experienced some form of sexual abuse as children.* And two-thirds of Mustang's prostitutes considered themselves religiously observant and professed membership in traditional organized faith communities, almost exclusively Protestant, Catholic, or Jewish.

It was clear that the women working in Nevada's brothels represented a distinct group. Fewer than half of Mustang's prostitutes had sold sex outside the brothels, whether "on the track" (the street) or through escort or outcall services. Although it wasn't unusual for streetwalkers to give Nevada brothels a try as a respite from the streets, George Flint figured that under 10 percent of the brothels' regular prostitutes were former streetwalkers. He speculated that the reason was the brothels' extensive rules and obligatory confinement: "True street girls can't make the adjustment. Every one of them fails. Maybe they're too accustomed to their independence. Or the fact that they choose their customers, their customers don't choose them."

One trait common to most of Mustang's women was financial hardship. Since Donna's husband was unemployable, or claimed to be, someone needed to earn a living for the family; she had only a high school education and meager work experience, and he convinced her she had few options. This

---

*U.S. Department of Health and Human Services, Administration on Children, Youth, and Families. *Child Maltreatment 1998: Reports From the States to the National Child Abuse and Neglect Data System* (Washington, D.C.: U.S. Government Printing Office, 2000).

was a pattern I saw frequently—women who had ended up at Mustang Ranch to provide for loved ones. Instead of lacking family values, as moralists contended, most of the women I came to know there possessed a profound sense of personal responsibility and an unwavering commitment to their families that ultimately drove them to do this "immoral" work.

Almost every woman was financially supporting someone else—often her husband, sometimes other family members. Carrie, a prostitute in her early thirties, was taking care of her mother, who had turned her out more than a decade ago. With raven-black hair down to her buttocks, Carrie bore an uncanny resemblance to Morticia Addams, a likeness enhanced by the black dress she always wore: tight-fitting, low-cut, long, and sheer. Forbidden to return home until she earned the quota her mother set, Carrie was frequently forced to remain at Mustang for weeks on end.

Then there was Ivy, whose mother-in-law had packed up her bags and loaded them in the car before announcing that she had freeloaded off her husband's family long enough—her mother-in-law was taking her to Mustang Ranch to get a job.

It wasn't always families that the women subsidized; all too frequently, pimp boyfriends had manipulated them. The women didn't admit this to me readily, however. In fact, the subject of pimps didn't come up until I met Brittany, a thirty-one-year-old with a sweet, wholesome face devoid of any makeup, and a pageboy haircut. Instead of the standard brothel "eye patch" bikini top, which barely covered the nipples, and matching "tulip" shorts, cut to expose both buttocks cheeks, Brittany stuck with knee-length cocktail dresses. I couldn't get over how much she resembled an old high school friend of mine. Brittany kept her distance from me for a couple of days, then approached me one afternoon in the Mustang bar. To break the ice, I asked her how the brothels had changed over the eleven years she had worked in them. She mentioned how the previously obligatory three weeks on/one week off work schedule had been relaxed, and how the house minimums had gone up from $30 when she started to $100. And of course, she said, the brothels used to require women to have pimps. Startled, I asked her to repeat herself. I had assumed one of the benefits of legalized prostitution was the elimination of pimps.

Realizing that no one had yet let me in on this well-kept dirty secret, Brittany reiterated that the brothels used to require women to have pimps before they were hired. The rationale was simple. The involvement of pimps enabled brothel owners to leave discipline to men who wouldn't hesitate to keep their women in line. Brittany said it wasn't unusual for an owner like Joe Conforte to collect all the pimps' phone numbers, and call them whenever a girl misbehaved to come "straighten her out real quick." All too frequently, Brittany said, "straightening out" involved brute force. Owners also benefited from the pimps' relentless demands that the women earn more and more money.

Meanwhile, pimps found much appeal in placing their prostitutes in Nevada's brothels, despite having to relinquish half of the women's earnings to owners. For one, the pimps could be assured their prostitutes would be supervised and attended to. Once extricated from the burdens inherent to managing working girls illegally, these men were free to seduce other women into the trade. A pimp could keep track of his prostitute's business simply by calling the brothel and speaking with the cashier or a manager, who freely disclosed the women's earnings. He frequently kept abreast of his prostitutes' daily conduct by putting all his working girls together in the same brothel and encouraging them to snitch on one another.

Even though the brothels no longer required women to have pimps, many of Mustang's working girls still did, confided Brittany in a hushed tone. How many women? I asked, incredulous. Brittany glanced quickly around the room and let out a sigh before replying that almost all the girls did, in her opinion. Those without pimps, she said, included herself, Baby, Dinah, and a few others. With disbelief, I briefly surveyed the room. Why on earth would these legal prostitutes need pimps? Off the unsafe streets, they surely didn't need a pimp's protection. Weren't the women already giving up a significant portion of their money to the house? The brothels functioned as stand-in pimps. Most of the women had portrayed themselves as tough and independent-minded women who viewed prostitution simply as a job, a way to earn a living. I hadn't detected any signs of coercion. And I had never heard any of the other women talking about pimps.

Brittany wasn't surprised to learn this. None of the women would've wanted to admit aloud to being exploited, to giving up their hard-earned money to a man when the brothel already extracted half their earnings. Moreover, Brittany said, most of these women denied that their pimps *were* pimps, considering them "boyfriends" and "friends." She had reason to know, she said; she'd once had a pimp herself. "God forbid if you ever called him a pimp. It wasn't even in your vocabulary. It was like a bad word," she said. "But as far as I'm concerned, if you're sending your money to a man who wouldn't be with you if you weren't sending him money, then he's not your boyfriend, he's your pimp. Still, it took me a year after I left Bobby to be able to call him my pimp."

By now, Brittany had settled into the bar stool next to me, completely absorbed in recounting her story, raising her voice occasionally to be heard over Marvin Gaye's "Let's Get It On" blasting from the jukebox. Whenever the doorbell rang, Brittany ducked her head below the counter of the bar so as not to be caught skipping lineup by Blanche, the floor maid. Brittany's behavior further substantiated my sense that management didn't actually respect women's status as independent contractors. I also wondered if brothel management would be angry with Brittany for revealing that owners once collaborated with pimps and fostered prostitutes' dependence upon them. Frankly, Brittany's candidness surprised me, especially if, as she said, having a pimp bore such a social stigma. It was as if Brittany wanted to get this secret off her chest and had picked me to bear witness.

Hers was the classic story of being caught by a pimp, she said. At the age of eighteen, shortly after graduating from a

Catholic high school, she met Bobby while working as a bank teller. He spent three months actively pursuing her, wining and dining her and lavishing her with bouquets and gifts, always acting the gentleman to win her affection. Brittany was flattered by all this attention from a thirty-year-old, and soon he had seduced her. Then one night over dinner, Bobby announced he needed some money—he had started running out—especially because of all he had spent wooing her. To maintain their standard of living, Brittany began charging their expenses and soon accrued a credit card bill of $20,000.

When she told Bobby of her debt, his response was a cold-blooded "How are you going to pay that off?" Then, for the first time, he mentioned prostitution. Specifically, he told her she should consider going to Nevada to work in a legal brothel. At first, Brittany adamantly refused. She had been raised in a religious family and could never sell her body. But over time, as her debt accumulated and Bobby kept encouraging her to prostitute, she began to waver. She didn't give in until he finally issued an ultimatum: either she start prostituting or he would leave her. "Why should I be with you if you're not doing anything for me?" he asked her. Afraid of losing him, Brittany finally submitted.

Using both guilt and the pretense of love, pimps baited and coaxed women to turn out, Brittany said. Sadly, they rarely reciprocated women's love in any genuine way. Brittany explained that pimps like Bobby typically used insincere promises of fidelity to placate their prostitutes while continuing to philander in attempts to catch and turn out additional women.

Most pimps strove to establish a stable of women off whom they could profit. By arranging for his prostitutes to work staggered three-week schedules in the brothels, so that only one would be home at any given time, a man could fool each woman into believing she was his one and only. Prostitutes who were aware of the existence of others competed ferociously to win their pimp's favor. Many pimps exacerbated the women's rivalry, pitting them against one another with the prospect that one prostitute would eventually win out and the two of them together would reap the benefits of all the other girls' work. There was even an expression for this coveted position: "bottom bitch."

But Brittany knew only one woman who had claimed victory and ended up with her pimp: her friend April, who had retired off the floor, or quit prostituting, thirteen years earlier and now worked as a night floor maid at Mustang Ranch. One night April opened up to me and confessed that even though she'd prevailed and had been married for over eighteen years to her former pimp, the road had been tough. "I was bitter about my experience," she said. "I couldn't forget those early years. It had been very difficult to share my man with other women. Even after we'd been out of the business and out of the life for a while, he was always looking to catch one girl and to keep her for a couple of months to make some quick money. I had a big problem with that because I didn't want to share him anymore."

More typically, relationships between prostitutes and pimps ended the way Brittany's had. After almost three years of financial exploitation and some physical abuse, Brittany finally admitted to herself that Bobby was using her. But when she announced her intention to part ways, Bobby said she would have to leave all her possessions behind, regardless of the fact that she had helped him amass eight cars, several homes, and jewelry. In the end, she said, she barely got out of their house with the clothes on her back. With nowhere else to go, nothing to show for her years of work, and not enough confidence to try anything else, Brittany returned to Nevada's brothels, only this time as an "outlaw," a prostitute without a pimp. She had been working independently now for nearly eight years.

Although the brothel industry no longer worked in collusion with pimps, Brittany felt outraged that owners and management didn't do more to rid the business of pimps altogether. Instead, the brothels maintained a hands-off policy, perhaps not wanting to deprive themselves of the constant supply of prostitutes still furnished by pimps. Law enforcement officials in Oregon, where for some reason many of today's West Coast pimps allegedly originate, estimate that pimps in the Eugene-Springfield area have over forty women working in Nevada's brothels who regularly send tens of thousands of dollars back home. When I asked George about this, the next time he drove out to Mustang to check on me, he downplayed it. Rather perfunctorily, he said it was a shame that the women had pimps, and it was nothing the brothel industry was proud of. He could no more understand why the women would give up their money to pimps, he said, than he could understand why the women tended to date ex-cons. (His question *was* a good one—why were some women emotionally vulnerable to such men and other women not?)

Brittany and the few others like her who had broken free of pimps tried to warn women who had them that they would eventually be left with nothing to show for their years of hard work. Occasionally, a woman took her colleagues' words to heart and left her pimp, but usually the efforts were futile. Once, I witnessed a couple of women trying to encourage a working girl named Monica to leave her "old man." He was one of two infamous twins from Oregon, Henry and Harold, black men in their late twenties or early thirties who "kept" thirteen or fourteen girls apiece, all almost identical. Monica typified the look with her tall, long-legged frame, blond hair, and fresh, cover-of-*Seventeen*-magazine face. The women shared something else: the twins had marked all of them with identical ankle tattoos.

The women tried to point out to Monica how cruel her pimp was; he forced her to work without a single day off for over five months. Didn't Monica see how he was using her? Monica resisted; Henry had trained her well. He loved her dearly, she insisted, and only wanted her to work hard so they could be together sooner. The two had plans to run away to California and start a family. When the women asked why Henry never seemed to want to see her, never visited her or flew her home to Oregon but still expected her Western Unions to be timely and bountiful, Monica started crying. Inside, she had obviously wondered the same thing. But she wouldn't dream of questioning Henry, she said, or she might lose him.

She didn't know what she would do without him. Wasn't it proof enough that he loved her, Monica asked hopefully, that he cried and begged her forgiveness after fights they had over the telephone? Deep down, she said, Henry needed her, and she didn't want to disappoint him.

Brittany contended that husbands like Donna's and men like Bobby and Henry and Harold were all pimps, period. Other women sharply disagreed; I found that whether or not their significant others should be regarded as pimps was a hotly contested topic among brothel prostitutes.

When Brittany had decided to get married, four years earlier, she was very careful. Even though her husband, Jon, unlike her former pimp, held a full-time job as an accounts manager for a manufacturing company, Brittany knew she could easily fall back into the same old role: "He says he'd never take advantage of me like that. But I tell him he wouldn't have to. I'd let him do it, because I've been in that role before—of giving, giving, giving. It's all I know how to do." Brittany refused to combine their incomes and insisted on splitting all bills 50–50. "There's no mooching. I don't send him my money or come home and hand him my purse. My money goes directly into my checking account, and I can spend as much as I want. He doesn't ask me about my money. I'm careful not to let him cross that line."

My long discussion with Brittany at the bar ended abruptly when one of her regulars found her sitting with me and asked to go back to her bedroom to "talk," the brothel euphemism for negotiating prices. As soon as Brittany walked away, I became aware of feeling empty. Knowing that so many of these women had been manipulated by men they loved cast them in a new, more tragic light. I felt sickened by the thought of such controlling, self-serving men, using these women who had sincere hopes of creating a plentiful, secure future for their loved ones.

I suddenly missed my home, and my husband (my fiancé and I married in 1994). How would I have felt if he had suggested I increase our family's income and give Mustang Ranch a try? I would have felt as if he'd sold me down the river. I suddenly felt desperate to call Andy. Wanting to stay immersed in the immediate experience, I hadn't called home much, but now I found myself homesick. Then I remembered it was Saturday night, when phone use in the brothel was forbidden. From six P.M. Friday until six A.M. Sunday, Mustang's phone room, a small room off the parlor with four pay phones—women's sole means of communication with the outside world—was locked. When the prostitutes griped, old-timers, like Blanche the floor maid, waxed on about how much more restrictive the phone rules used to be: back in the 1970s, women were allowed two incoming and two outgoing phone calls per week, and no calls were permitted between four P.M. and nine P.M. Phone prohibitions had always been justified on the grounds that news from home frequently disrupted women's ability to concentrate on the job.

Indeed, I had seen that happen. I'd seen Baby storm out of Mustang to patch things up with her boyfriend of eight months after he gave her an ultimatum over the phone: quit the business immediately or he would leave her. I'd heard Tanya screaming into the telephone receiver at her husband almost loud enough to be heard back in the bedrooms: "Here I am trying to make some money for us. I don't want to just make minimum payments on our J. C. Penney's, Montgomery Ward, and Chase credit cards. Don't you want enough money to do the things we've been talking about doing? You're not doing your part. Ever since your brother came around all you do— all you think about—is getting to a bar. You're going to become an alcoholic."

Even I was bickering more with my husband the few times we had spoken. While I wanted to share all that I was seeing, I felt protective of this world, and I found myself impatient when he failed to respond as I wanted him to. At the same time, I wasn't really that interested in what was happening to him in his world. I hung up many times feeling more alone than I had before I called.

Some of the women apparently felt the same way; I observed that they tried to minimize contact with home during the weeks they worked at Mustang. In fact, a few women didn't talk to their families at all from the brothel. Those who had pimps, by contrast, were harassed and checked up on throughout the day. When the women did talk to home, they were generally unforthcoming about what was happening at work, for fear of upsetting their husbands or lovers. Brothel prostitutes ended up keeping their workplace stresses to themselves. Almost no one discussed the sex they had with customers, with the exception of a prostitute who told me that her husband, a U.S. Immigration and Naturalization Service agent, was aroused by stories of her sexual encounters with customers.

Although Donna's husband originally claimed that he wouldn't be bothered by her having sex with strange men, she learned early on that he wasn't as indifferent as he had professed to be. "It was all so new, all the different types of sexual experiences men wanted; I only knew about oral sex and straight sex," Donna confessed sheepishly to me one day. "Of course, I wanted to chat about all of it with him; he was my best friend, the only person who knew what I was doing, the only person I could talk to. I can't remember what I said one evening, but he gave me this look of disgust and said he didn't want to hear about what I did to these other guys. Then he changed the subject, and I knew right then and there that I'd never mention anything ever again. And he's never asked." This was the only way, Donna said, that her husband could cope with her work. I was skeptical, however, that a husband could effectively block out the knowledge that his wife was having sex with other men.

I had a chance to judge for myself when I met Brittany's husband. Out of nowhere one day, she invited me to join them in Reno for dinner after she finished her shift, her last before a vacation. She claimed she wanted to prove to me that Jon really wasn't a quasi-pimp.

When Jon walked into Mustang that night to pick us up, the women initially mistook him for a trick. Within minutes, two working girls had accosted and propositioned him. Blushing, Jon laughed and explained that he was there to see Brittany. As soon as she emerged from her bedroom, where she'd been with a customer, she spotted him waiting alone in the bar and rushed over to greet him. Self-conscious, they didn't kiss publicly but just nuzzled for a few minutes. Then Brittany led Jon over to the parlor couch where I was sitting, to introduce us and ask if I was ready to go.

En route to dinner in their brand-new Ford Explorer, I asked him what it felt like to walk into Mustang and see Brittany working. Before he had time to answer, Brittany interrupted to say that he never saw the customers; he blocked them out. Jon agreed, and added that he was just relieved that the facility wasn't a flophouse, scummy and dirty with cockroaches and people shooting up drugs in the corner—in short, the typical caricature of the prostitute's world.

Our conversation continued in that vein through dinner. A tall, attractive man in his early forties with bleached blond hair and a face that reminded me of Sting, Jon was remarkably, well, normal appearing. I was struck by how protective he was of Brittany, and how obliging he was of me. Having been warned by Brittany that I would probably bombard him with questions, Jon sat patiently and answered me earnestly. When I asked him how he blocked out the customers, he admitted that he had been very inquisitive at the beginning of their relationship, asking Brittany a lot of questions in an attempt to understand her experience. In particular, he needed to know how she kept from becoming emotionally involved with customers, especially if the men were "really good in bed." "I would never tell him anything descriptive or graphic," Brittany put in. "He didn't need to have visuals. My answers were very vague and simple."

Jon said that Brittany had put him at ease when she described her standard technique for emotionally detaching from her clients during sex. "I didn't understand what she meant when she said that she could separate from her work. Then she explained how she disconnects and doesn't feel anything. She said she sees blackness and nothingness where the man's face should be." Jon decided to challenge himself to master Brittany's technique of repressing the reality of her work. "I asked myself, What am I, a wimp, because I can't block it out and she can? I've learned not to think about what she does. She sells things. She's a salesperson just like I'm a salesperson. She doesn't know necessarily what I sell, and I don't necessarily know what she sells. I see nothing else and I just don't dwell on it." Still, every couple of days Jon felt compelled to call Brittany on the brothel pay phones to ask her to tell him once again how much she loved him.

Meanwhile, Brittany admitted, she wasn't sure how she wanted Jon to feel about her work. Women who, like Brittany, had been in the business long before meeting their current partners, often harbored conflicting desires—wanting their lovers both to hate and to respect their professional choices. Brittany wanted Jon to tell her to stop working, yet didn't want him to encroach upon her independence. "While I want him to try to get me to quit, I wouldn't respect him if he did. That means messing up *my* money. But I also wouldn't want him to be indifferent or not to care."

Jon had learned his lesson about two years earlier, when he decided to put his foot down and refuse to share his wife with strangers any longer. Deprived of her source of financial security, Brittany grew increasingly anxious, until finally Jon reconsidered. "I guess if I had the opportunity as a man to make the money some of these women do," he said, "if I tasted the kind of money some of these women make, I'd have trouble suddenly giving it up, too. She wants to build a nest egg for our family."

What did bother Jon was the effect Brittany's work had on their sex life. Burned out physically and mentally, she had difficulty becoming sexual immediately upon returning home from a stint in the brothels. Needing to acclimate, she often preferred to catch up on sleep instead. Even after several days, she sometimes had no interest in sex and favored cuddling and talking. Although he was usually frustrated after they had been apart, sometimes for weeks, Jon said he tried to be understanding and to leave Brittany alone until she made the first move.

To add to Jon's difficulties, Brittany was uncomfortable initiating sex, having come to associate that responsibility with her role as a prostitute. "I have to literally coach myself in my head that this is my husband and that I can get into it," she said, glancing nervously over at Jon to watch his reaction. "Sometimes it offends me because I know he wants sex. I don't mean to, but all my defenses come up. As soon as he starts becoming sexual, I become almost frigid!" While Brittany spoke, Jon didn't lift his eyes off his plate, empty now save for a few cold French fries and a couple of colored toothpicks that had decorated his club sandwich. He looked as if he had just had the wind knocked out of him.

I was surprised by Brittany's response. To the extent that I'd considered the matter at all, I assumed that an advantage of being a professional prostitute was learning precisely how to please a man, and thus developing great sexual self-confidence. In reality, many of the Mustang prostitutes, like Brittany, confessed that they had grown sexually repressed and inhibited at home since beginning their careers.

Women also described needing specific sexual activities to become sufficiently aroused: prolonged kissing, foreplay, fantasizing, dirty talk, loving words, and for some, intoxication. "He can't take off his clothes and stand in front of me naked because it reminds me too much of work and all the other men I see standing there like that," said Brittany. "He has to move slowly and we have to do special things, like take a shower together or play with our clothes on for a while, otherwise it's too much like work." Still, most of the women working at Mustang—including Brittany—said they had sexually satisfying relationships with their lovers. Over 90 percent of the women told me they orgasmed with their lovers, and almost half said they did so every time.

After a few minutes of silence, Jon said that he had long sensed Brittany's inhibition but hoped it would dissipate over time. What bothered him even more was her opposition to having children. Brittany couldn't face the possibility of her kids finding out that she had worked as a prostitute. "Do I want to have to explain to my children what I have done for more than a decade?" Brittany snapped. Somberly, she added, "It makes me very sad, because I love children. There are a lot of girls that have babies, but the price seems too high to pay." Working lawfully, as a licensed prostitute, didn't seem to eliminate the shame associated with prostitution. Jon responded that he would defend Brittany's past choices, if she agreed to quit working should she ever have children.

But many of Mustang's prostitutes, like Donna, worked despite having children at home. In fact, over one-third of the women who worked at Mustang Ranch were mothers. As Brittany suspected, however, the sacrifices were significant. Licensed prostitutes couldn't go home at the end of the day to cook their children dinner or tuck them into bed. Often away for weeks at a time, they had to rely on others to look after their kids—lovers, family, or friends. Irene, the manager at #2, confided that she found this one of the saddest aspects of the job. She always warned new applicants just how limited their contact with their children would be. "Given that this isn't a nine-to-five job and they can't just run home, I ask how they've planned for an emergency, who has the authority to take their children to the hospital if they get sick."

Women tried to make it up to their kids with regular telephone calls, letters, and material objects. With their newly earned cash, prostitutes frequently paid the brothel runners to go on shopping sprees in local toy stores before the women left for home on vacation. The runners would return looking like Santa Claus, bearing shopping bags filled with hundreds of dollars' worth of toys, from Barbie dolls and

Beanie Babies to sneakers and video games. The overspending seemed so extreme, I couldn't help but think it reflected the women's effort to assuage their guilt and win their children's affection.

Donna was no different. One day I saw her bustling about, trying to decide what she should bring home to her kids on her weeklong vacation. She had already sent the runner out to Toys "R" Us to start stocking up. When Amber the "candy lady" stopped in, Donna rushed back to the kitchen to buy some additional treats. One of several door-to-door vendors who brought their wares to the brothel, Amber always came prepared. She knew that many of the women relied on her for presents for their families.

Unlike some of the other vendors, who serviced Mustang Ranch weekly, Amber drove in from California to sell her homemade confectionery only every couple of months, usually around holidays like Halloween, Christmas, and Valentine's Day. On this particular visit, two weeks before Father's Day, she was offering chocolates molded into neckties and tool sets. But she also always had candy for children: dark, milk, and white chocolate in animal shapes from rabbits to dinosaurs. Amber's prices ranged from $8 to $25 for individually boxed candy. On this particular day, Donna bought a hundred dollars' worth of chocolate for her two children.

In addition to chocolates and toys, Donna always brought home make-believe stories about her job as a stewardess. There was the tale of meeting Michael Jordan on a flight to Chicago, and the one about helping the pilot land the plane. It was common for the mothers to make up lies to explain their absences. In fact, most of the women, mothers or not, led double lives, keeping their profession secret from extended family and friends. What struck me was that most women told stories that were *almost* true. Savannah told her in-laws she sold phone sex on a 900 number. Lara told her mother that her large all-cash income came from selling drugs. I found it fascinating that phone sex and drug dealing seemed all that less objectionable than prostitution. Savannah explained that she wished she could tell her family the truth but feared rejection, and that telling partial truths felt better than blatantly lying. Feeling compelled to lie only reinforced the shame of prostitution.

I was greatly surprised one morning, then, when the mother of a prostitute named Jasmine rang the doorbell at Mustang #1 with Jasmine's two young sons, aged five and eight, in tow to pick up money for the household. When the grandmother and boys were admitted through Mustang's gates, Jasmine rushed out to the front yard to greet them. The boys didn't blink at their mother's electric-pink hot pants; they were much more interested in the Popsicles another woman brought out for them. As Jasmine and her mother spoke, another prostitute chased the two children around the yard in a game of tag. The presence of these merry and energetic children transformed the entire brothel, giving it the cheerful atmosphere of a playground.

Still, I found it jarring to see young children hanging around a brothel while men continued to ring the bell and pass through the gates. By law, people under eighteen weren't allowed on brothel property, and the floor maid came outside to make sure Jasmine knew the boys would absolutely not be permitted inside. Later, Jasmine told me that her sons knew that their mother worked at the "famous" Mustang Ranch, but had no idea what the Ranch really was. I wondered how long it would be before they understood.

What had the children thought of the fortresslike eight-foot fence behind which their mother worked? What had Jasmine's mother felt on seeing her daughter dressed up in her working outfit? When the time finally came for the boys to leave, they burst into tears and had to be pulled from Jasmine's side by their grandmother, who promised them a Happy Meal at McDonald's if they would "just get into the fucking car." When the blue Oldsmobile finally pulled away, I caught Jasmine wiping a tear from her eye.

What hard choices these women made. It was a brutal calculus of sacrifices made for the large incomes most of them enjoyed. But isn't ours a culture that reveres those who earn big, fast money? We don't commend the women holding down two blue-collar jobs. We fail to adequately compensate or applaud social workers, teachers, and housecleaners. Weren't the prostitutes doing what moralists have long preached? They weren't looking for handouts or freeloading off the system.

And they took their work seriously. Not only were they committed to earning a decent livelihood, but many of the working girls I met at Mustang Ranch tried genuinely to meet the demands and needs of their customers. Their dedication amazed me. I was still having trouble imagining being courteous and social with some of these men, to say nothing of sleeping with them. How did the women feel about the work they did? How did they bear it?

4 .. PRIDE IN ONE'S WORK

"I have a thing for large breasts," I overheard a young man whisper almost apologetically to Blanche, the floor maid on duty at Mustang #1. The customer, a man in his late twenties wearing a beat-up aviator jacket, his hair pulled back in a loose ponytail that hung down between his shoulder blades, had come to the brothel alone. He had stood through the lineup and was disappointed with what was on offer. "I mean *extremely* large breasts," he said, thrusting his hands out to make the point.

The floor maid turned her head to the women standing in line. "Thank you, ladies," she said, excusing them.

As the women broke from lineup, a few of them made faces of disgust, irritation, and annoyance at the waste of time;

the rest calmly returned to whatever they had been doing before the doorbell rang. The women killed time between customers the way people kill time everywhere: smoking, snacking, crocheting, gossiping, napping, reading, and playing cards. House rules forbade them from doing any of these things when customers were in the parlor.

Blanche turned back to the young man at her side, who was nervously fidgeting with the zipper of his jacket. The brothel's most buxom working girl, Lynn, was busy with another customer, she said, but shouldn't be much longer. She ushered him over to an empty couch to wait.

Lynn was one of Mustang's veterans, a woman in her forties with huge, ponderous, water-balloon breasts, which she showed off with plunging necklines. She used her revealing clothes and a large collection of pornography devoted to busty women to entice customers with breast fetishes. When she finally emerged from her room about twenty minutes later, the young man leaped to his feet and broke into a wide grin of satisfaction.

Customer obsessions like this no longer startled me. In a relatively short time, I had seen a wide array of men come through Mustang Ranch with an equally wide array of predilections. About 200,000 men visited Mustang Ranch's two brothels annually, accounting for fully half of Nevada's brothel business. They were businessmen, conventioneers, fraternity brothers, truckers, hardhats, oil and mineral drilling crews, migrant farmers, disabled veterans, traveling salesmen, bachelor party guests, politicians, and even nationally known celebrities. One evening, a busload of fifteen Japanese tourists on an organized sex tour filed in, accompanied by a tour guide acting as interpreter. The men's tastes all differed, so nearly every prostitute managed to "break," the word for having at least one customer daily. Some of Mustang's customers wanted breasts, others buttocks. Many preferred blondes, others demanded brunettes. Some sought out the raunchiest-dressed women, and still others looked for the girl next door.

Men's manners ran the gamut as well. Most were courteous, but others were blatantly rude. Some men walked up to within inches of the women in lineup, breathing heavily and slowly giving each the once-over as if she were a mannequin. Within earshot of the women, one cocky frat boy muttered to his buddies, "Don't they have anything pretty in here?" The women stood stoically as the floor maid snapped that maybe he needed some taste. Other men came into Mustang and walked right past the lineup to the bar as if oblivious to the women standing at attention for their benefit. "Do they stand like that all the time?" a customer mumbled incredulously to his pal. "Oh, yeah, we stand here like plastic dolls for your entertainment," one of the women shot back.

Frankly, I hadn't really expected the men to behave well. I always assumed that any man who would patronize a brothel and buy sex from a prostitute believed deep down that women were commodities. Most of the prostitutes were unfazed by bad behavior; they'd seen and heard it all before. Most understood that customers' rudeness was usually a front for insecurity, fear, and embarrassment. The lineup, especially, could be an intimidating moment for even the most self-confident of men. Ironically, that brief moment of deciding which prostitute to pick was a man's only real moment of power in the brothel. After that, the women seized control, determining what type of sex would be made available and at what price. A man who behaved like a pig in the parlor was guaranteed to pay inflated prices in the bedroom, both as a punishment and as compensation for the anticipated additional work needed to tolerate him.

Some of the men tried to act gentlemanly; they bought the women drinks, asked them about their interests, and tried to establish a rapport. Because business negotiations and explicit sexual talk were prohibited outside the bedrooms, these preliminary exchanges amounted to superficial small talk.

The women's work in the parlor and bar had become almost routine to me now, but once the women walked out of the parlor and headed to their bedrooms with the men in tow, I was left to my imagination. I understood that the prostitutes needed to negotiate prices, examine the men's penises, and put condoms on, but I didn't know how they choreographed all this. And as for the sex, I couldn't imagine it as anything but mechanical, dispassionate, and impersonal, like the quickies homeless teens sold on the streets of Times Square.

But maybe not. Mustang Ranch was very different from the fleabag motels, cars, and alleyways used by street prostitutes. The working girls here had their own private, personally decorated rooms. In fact, many of them had done up their rooms elaborately with fancy wallpaper, curtains, and light fixtures. On the walls hung posters of women's favorite musicians and movies, *Playboy* centerfolds and *Sports Illustrated* swimsuit calendars.

But the women went back with up to twelve men per shift: it was hard to imagine sex not becoming mechanical. And the challenge of having to cope with some men's bad behavior was equaled by that of needing to tolerate others' personal hygiene. Gene, for example, a Mustang regular, always wore the same soiled jeans, torn, rank baseball jersey, and dingy baseball cap; he chain-smoked down to the filter and scattered the ashes everywhere. Most women kept a row of cleaning products in the bathroom to wash down the toilet seat, bidet, and shower after each client, a grim necessity. Then there were the drunks who threw up and passed out on the women—a not infrequent occurrence.

One day, I caught a glimpse of sex between a brothel prostitute and her customer. I had gone down to my room to use the toilet and found my bathmate's door slightly ajar. It was early afternoon and her room was dark, so I assumed she wasn't inside and went to pull the door shut. As I reached for the handle, I heard soft murmurs coming from inside the room. I froze in place and held my breath. As I leaned forward to listen more closely, figuring it was just two working girls gossiping, it suddenly registered. It was my bathmate and a customer!

Shamelessly, I pushed open her door a crack more. All was dark except for a red lightbulb in the table lamp, which threw a soft, warm glow over the bed. There, two pairs of bare legs were entwined and rolling back and forth. The couple's movement was natural and fluid. Instead of being stiff and awkward, the sex looked soft and gentle, almost intimate. I stared for a few seconds before creeping away.

Later that night, I found myself alone with Baby, and I told her what I had seen. I said I was taken aback to see that sex between a prostitute and her customer could be so tender. Baby smiled. That was the prostitute's *job*, she said: to act, to satisfy the sexual desires and fantasies of all her customers. Not all clients wanted hard, impersonal sex, she pointed out. Many wanted soft lovemaking. Others had more specific needs. There was Hangman Harvey, a necrophiliac, who paid Mustang prostitutes to pretend to be dead during intercourse. Or the man with AIDS who turned up at Mustang Ranch searching only for kindness and compassion. The prostitute who serviced him recalled, "He announced to everybody that he had AIDS and didn't want to have sex. He said that everybody had been treating him badly since they found out he had AIDS. He just needed somebody to talk to, some companionship, and some human touch. I gave him a long backrub."

The men were as various as their demands. There were the "normal" men seeking types of sex unavailable to them at home or elsewhere, like fellatio or cunnilingus. One thirty-year-old drove over seven hundred miles from his California home to have sex in the brothels because of his girlfriend's vow to remain "as pure as the driven snow" until marriage. One of Baby's many regulars was a professional golfer who was afraid he would scare away his longtime girlfriend if he requested the rough sex he felt comfortable asking for only from a prostitute. There were workaholics too busy to invest time in relationships, and commitment-resistant men who craved sex unfettered by responsibilities or obligations. And of course, there were always the men desperate to lose their virginity.

I met one of these the day he came in with his father. The boy was a tall, gangly adolescent dressed in typical slept-in-looking teen garb—loose-fitting jeans, rumpled plaid shirt, sneakers, and a baseball cap. Underneath his cap, his eyes darted about frantically; he was very tightly wound. The boy, whose name was Zachary, didn't choose a woman out of the lineup; he remained quiet as his father started grilling one of the prostitutes seated on a couch, Keri, about how the brothel worked. Suddenly, in the middle of one of his father's questions, Zachary stood up and indicated that he was ready to go back to the room with Keri. Watching from the sidelines on a different parlor couch, I wondered if the boy actually wanted to go or was just trying to get his father to stop talking. "You'll take care of him, won't you?" his father called out to Keri as she led Zachary away.

As soon as Zachary was gone, his father let out an audible sigh of relief and pulled out a *Time* magazine from his Patagonia jacket. Although he tried to appear engrossed in the text, I caught him scanning the parlor every couple of minutes to check out the scene. Interested in why a father would bring his son to Mustang Ranch, I went over to introduce myself. He assumed I was a prostitute coming to hit on him. "I'm really not interested, miss," he said. He was only there for his nineteen-year-old son, he said. They were en route to Las Vegas for a little "R and R." When I explained that I wasn't a prostitute, he relaxed a bit and slowly began to tell the real story.

A college freshman on the East Coast, Zachary had recently suffered a psychological breakdown, characterized by delusions and auditory hallucinations. Zachary had had a rough first semester, his father explained, being three thousand miles away from home and having to make new friends. His father attributed his psychological break to an adjustment disorder, along with the fact that Zachary had found himself the brunt of his peers' jokes for still being a virgin. After watching a segment featuring Mustang Ranch on *60 Minutes*, his father decided that this would be the safest and surest way for his son to lose his virginity and, he hoped, remedy the entire situation.

Although he was professionally successful and obviously intelligent, Zachary's father was clearly in denial about his son's condition. Given Zachary's age and symptoms, it seemed likely that he had schizophrenia, an illness that certainly couldn't be cured simply by losing one's virginity. I felt for Zachary's father, who was so desperate to fix his son's problems that he was grasping at straws, flying his son out to a legal brothel in Nevada despite moral reservations. But I felt much more for Zachary, and wondered what his mother thought about this solution. In focusing on the issue of sex, Zachary's father assigned epic proportions to his son's virginity.

Keri told me later that she'd picked up on this pressure immediately. Zachary hadn't told her about his breakdown but instead simply said that he was being mocked for being a virgin and this was his chance to prove his manhood. Unfortunately, he did not lose his virginity that day. Despite Keri's concerted efforts and even a generous extension of time—she kept him in her room for sixty minutes rather than the usual thirty to forty—Zachary couldn't do it. "I tried and tried and tried," she told me. "He couldn't get hard. He was just so nervous. His legs were all tensed up."

Keri told Zachary that virgins frequently had trouble their first time because of nerves, and that many who came to Mustang were still virgins when they walked out the door. Still, no matter how she tried to comfort him, she knew he had left feeling inadequate. "He asked me not to tell his dad." She wondered whether Zachary might be worse off now, given the pressure imposed by his father. I, too, wondered how damaging this experience would be for the boy.

Keri was one of the few prostitutes who actually liked virgins. Most of the other women viewed them as stingy and labor-intensive. "Even though they're more work, I feel like I can provide an important service. I believe a man's first sexual experience shapes the way he treats women in the future. You can show him how a woman expects to be treated or touched. It's setting a standard for the rest of their life. I think it's going to help some woman down the line who deserves to be treated well by her man."

Hoping I wouldn't offend, I admitted to Keri that the idea of a young man losing his virginity to a stranger struck me as sad. I wished for him to share his first sexual experience with someone he cared about. But that wasn't about to happen for

Zachary, Keri reminded me. His peers were teasing him merci-
lessly. Anyway, she said, look how many boys hurry to lose
their virginity with anyone willing, any available one-night
stand. She had a point, of course. Perhaps there was something
to be said from learning to become an excellent lover from an
expert.

When I told Keri about Zachary's recent psychiatric history, her face fell. She already felt bad enough. While she had
attributed his problem to performance anxiety, Keri said she
also couldn't help but feel guilty. "When this happens with
customers, I almost feel like there's something wrong with me.
That *I'm* not good enough." Keri's sensitivity caught me off
guard. I hadn't imagined that prostitutes would see a client's
inability to climax as a personal failure. But Keri wasn't the
only one to express this sentiment to me.

In fact, most of the women took their work very seriously,
and many expressly considered it a form of social service on
par with others. Savannah told me she'd started prostituting at
Mustang as a social science experiment, to generate material
for her undergraduate thesis, and had recognized almost immediately just how meaningful prostitution could be. "I believe what I do is a healing job. I didn't see it as healing at first,
but I kept getting clients who just needed to be nurtured
and to weep in my arms. Sex is just the tool to access these
emotions. So I just hold these men and contemplate the psychological needs that drive them into my charge. The humanity
of my clients is what I care about." Considering herself a
professional therapist, Savannah fashioned specialty sessions

for impotent men, emphasizing sensate focus (a term used by sex therapists to describe the use of touch to convey sensory and eventually erotic pleasure) to gradually sensitize them to touch.

It came as no surprise, then, that when asked what other careers they would want to pursue, Savannah and most of Mustang's other prostitutes mentioned social work, nursing, teaching, day care: helping professions. In light of the fact that the majority of women prostituted for financial reasons, it was notable that they didn't aspire to big-money careers but were interested in work notorious for its low earning potential. One prostitute told me she was a nurse moonlighting at Mustang Ranch since her primary job failed to pay all her bills.

Perspectives like this kept women from fully internalizing disparaging remarks about prostitution. The women of Mustang Ranch were strikingly apolitical: untroubled and unreflective about whether prostitution dehumanized, demeaned, or objectified them, or about the larger social ramifications of selling their bodies to men. Initially, I assumed this was merely denial and avoidance on their part, but as I began inquiring further it became clear that the women had found a genuine sense of purpose and meaning in their work.

With this sense of purpose came real pride. The night I confessed to Baby about spying on my bathmate, she spoke with dignity about her job: "Prostitution doesn't need to be demeaning, done without self-respect. It's a very intimate, service-oriented, people-oriented profession. I feel what I do, I do good. Of all the customers I've had in my room, I would say at least ninety-seven point three percent of them have gotten off. I guess I feel, Be the best you can be at whatever you do. This is my career, and I have decided to excel at it. Granted, not everyone dreams of becoming a prostitute, but it has served me well." I was impressed by her sense of honest vocation, but I held on to my core skepticism.

Sensing that, Baby made me an extraordinary offer. Did I want to watch one of her sessions with a customer? She could show me what sex with a client was really all about. To watch a session between a working girl and a customer was the only way to truly understand and appreciate the work of a prostitute, she said.

I sat speechless. How would that be possible? Were there one-way mirrors somewhere in the brothel? Did she plan to hide me in her closet or the bathroom? What if I got caught? Would management throw me out? The brothel's priority was to satisfy the customer; my spying, a violation of the men's privacy, could certainly tick some of them off. I couldn't ask George to authorize this request. Did I even *want* to watch? Would I feel uncomfortable? Embarrassed? Sickened? I tried to tell myself it couldn't be much different from watching a porn movie.

I'm still not entirely sure what motivated Baby to let me watch. She knew I was interested in the workings of the industry and she had made it clear that she wanted to help educate me. More than that, though, she was *excited* about the idea of me watching her—as if she wanted the validation of my seeing how skilled she was at satisfying her customers. While women sometimes did "doubles" (parties with a customer and two prostitutes, or ménages à trois) and could watch each other work, Baby had never had the opportunity to impress a curious outsider. She was eager to show off her talents as a prostitute and to be respected as a professional. Her excitement was moving, and I felt I had little choice but to say yes.

For the rest of the week, I felt a surge of nervous energy each time a customer chose Baby out of lineup. Because the women debriefed each other in the parlor about their sessions with customers, I had some sense of what a typical party entailed. The most frequently requested party, fellatio plus intercourse, they called a half and half. The second most popular, simply fellatio, they called a total French. And one of the most expensive parties women sold, a "kitty licker" session, was one in which they let men perform oral sex on them.*

One night, Baby and I were chatting together in the parlor when Farrah, a working girl who looked eerily like Farrah Fawcett, crept up and whispered something into Baby's ear. Baby nodded and Farrah melted away as quickly as she had appeared. Baby turned to me and said, "Farrah has a guy who wants a dominance party. She doesn't know how to do the party so she's pulled me in." In brothel-speak, to be pulled into a party is to be included in a date with another woman's customer. It wasn't uncommon for less experienced women to try to pull in more experienced prostitutes like Baby, especially for specialty sessions like dominance.

---

*Before the mandatory-condom law, a number of customers requested a variation on kitty licking. "Load-eaters" were men who liked to perform cunnilingus on a prostitute immediately after another client had ejaculated into her vagina. Today, men who get off on drinking other men's semen must settle for buying used condoms, $50–$100 apiece, dug out of wastebaskets.

Baby hesitated for a moment. "So, I was thinking, maybe I can pull you in, too." As she said the words, I felt a rush of exhilaration and terror that almost nauseated me. Who knew when I'd have another chance to watch paid sex between a brothel prostitute and a customer? And this was no standard party. Dominance was one of the kinkiest activities sold. I nodded my assent. I'd come this far. Baby stood up and pulled down her tight spandex dress. She told me to stay in the parlor until she had arranged everything. Under no circumstances should I mention the plan to anyone, particularly Shelley the floor maid, who happened to be on duty and might fire Baby if she got wind of this.

Shelley was the ex-sadist who had bullied me my first day at Mustang #1. Although I'd made several visits to the brothel, I had yet to win her over. By now I had gotten used to her icy, suspicious stares. She had pulled Baby aside one day and told her to "be careful" around me; she accused Baby of divulging too many "industry secrets." The other women speculated that Shelley had a crush on Baby and was simply jealous of all the time I was spending with her. And in fact, when I finally confronted Shelley and asked her what she thought about me, she snarled, "I just think you're in love with Baby."

It was remarkable how often relationships became sexualized in the brothels. It was therefore no coincidence that both Shelley and I had been accused of lusting after Baby. While most of the relationships between women did have an unusual air of sexualized energy, very few of the prostitutes identified themselves as bisexual or lesbian. Although some women did have sex with other women in the brothel, almost all of them thought of themselves as heterosexuals who had merely been experimenting. "We are so isolated and lonely," said one woman. "I think we start looking for comfort and affection anywhere we can find it." Frankly, I was surprised that liaisons between women didn't occur more frequently, especially given the intense, concentrated time they spent pent up together. Anyway, whatever Shelley's true motives, I had no intention of telling *anyone* that I might get to be a voyeur.

While Baby was gone, I sat on the couch, my mind racing. Maybe this party would take place in Mustang's dungeon, a windowless, closet-sized room at the back of the brothel equipped with metal D-rings where women could attach various restraints like harnesses, chains, and cuffs. Would the man go all-out for whipping and beating? I had heard the women talk about a customer who wanted to be shocked with a cattle prod and another who asked to be locked in a doghouse for over twenty-four hours. One day while sitting in the parlor, I had seen a man brought out naked, leashed, and on all fours, like a dog. As I mulled over the stories I had heard about dominance parties, it suddenly struck me that Baby had used the expression "pull you in" rather vaguely. I hoped she didn't intend that I participate. But Baby had also said they would probably blindfold the man, I tried to reassure myself, in which case he probably wouldn't even know I was in the room.

Baby reappeared about fifteen minutes later and told me to follow her discreetly down to Farrah's room. As she led me down the hallway, she said Farrah hadn't quite gotten it right. Rather than whips and chains, this man wanted, in his own words, "to be taken anally" with a dildo. He had had this fantasy for some time but was too ashamed to ask any of his girlfriends to do it. Baby said it would be their responsibility to make him feel normal and acceptable in having this fantasy. As I tried to absorb this, she dropped a bombshell. "The customer is all right with you watching," she said as we reached the door to Farrah's room, "but he won't be wearing a blindfold. He wants to watch you watching him." With that, she threw open the door to Farrah's room.

Before me lay a boyish-looking man in his mid-thirties, stark naked on top of the bed. (Most of the women prohibited customers from getting underneath their sheets and comforters and had them lie on a top sheet, changed with each client.) When the customer saw me, he broke into a wide self-conscious grin that made his entire face squish up like an apple-face doll. "This is the girl I was telling you about," said Baby. "She's in training here. She's just going to watch. Farrah and I are going to get naked, not her." I breathed a sigh of relief.

Baby told me to take a seat on a nearby chair while she went to strap on the dildo. Meanwhile, Farrah sat at the head of the bed, massaging the client's back with her bare breasts. The man kept his eyes glued on Baby's image in a mirror hanging low on the wall as she buckled the thick leather dildo harness around her slender waist. When she began to roll the condom onto the dildo, the blond boy-man looked apprehensive for the first time.

His name was Jack, he told me later, and he was an

architect from southern California who was in town for a convention and had mustered up the courage to venture out to Mustang Ranch after a few cocktails in the casinos. He'd never expected to stay, but when he overheard some of the women in the brothel bar trading stories about some of the kinky as well as conventional kinds of sex they sold, he decided to take the plunge. Since his teens, Jack had suppressed his fantasy for fear of ridicule.

He had picked Farrah from lineup because she reminded him of one of the cheerleaders he had fantasized about in high school. Scared to put his desire into words, Jack became even more nervous after he had done so, when Farrah announced that she would have to check whether she could provide the service he wanted. Left alone in her bedroom, he considered getting dressed and scurrying out of the brothel to avoid the humiliation of being denied. But then Baby came in, having already assumed the persona of a dominatrix, and put him immediately at ease. Of course she knew what he wanted, she told him. He would just need to be a very good boy, or Miss Baby wouldn't give him what he deserved. She remained professional throughout the interaction, and in the process gave this man every indication that his sexual fantasy was normal and commonly requested. Her commanding but nonjudgmental demeanor permitted him to begin feeling aroused.

Undressed now down to a lacy black bra and a matching G-string beneath the strap-on, Baby spread open Jack's legs and let his knees hang off the bed before she began to penetrate him slowly from her standing position, her thighs pressed firmly against the bed. Jack winced as Baby forced the dry, condom-covered dildo into him, meeting significant resistance. (He had requested painful penetration.) Meanwhile, Farrah sat naked at the head of the bed, where Jack used his outstretched hands to play with her nipples while she occasionally slapped him across the hands. She looked uncomfortable in the twisted position necessary to give Jack access to her breasts and allow her simultaneously to observe what Baby was doing. With a better sense of Jack's tolerance for pain now, Baby began thrusting deeper into him, with the force of all her body weight.

"You like this don't you, bitch?" she roared, spanking him on the buttocks with an open hand. "You whore. You slut."

Intermittently, Baby took hold of Jack's testicles and squeezed them, making him yelp. Then she grabbed a tuft of his hair and yanked his head backward with a deliberate measure of control. She had achieved a perfect balance between violation and restraint—a controlled dominance, if you will—in which Jack felt safe enough to submit to the abuse willingly.

I noticed Jack's gaze in the reflection in the mirror. His self-conscious, goofy grin had evolved into a grimace that conveyed both his physical pain and psychological ecstasy. His wild eyes revealed his wonder at finally having his sexual fantasy realized in such a public way.

"Look at you beaming," Baby said contemptuously. "You like her watching, don't you? You think you're a little princess, don't you? You exhibitionist." While Baby said she saw him beaming, I saw him bursting with an electrified agony.

After almost ten minutes, Baby flipped Jack onto his back like a helpless animal. As she started thrusting into him again, this time with his legs draped over her shoulders, she began brusquely rubbing his very erect penis with a free hand. Baby was a master choreographer, acutely sensitive to the exact degree and extent of dominance called for. Jack was now panting like a dog and it took only a few strokes before he let out a howl and ejaculated all over his torso. (Condoms were not always used for hand jobs.)

The room was still for several minutes. Jack lay motionless, with his eyes closed. Silently, Baby and Farrah began moving about, putting the room back in order. Finally, Baby roused Jack with a gentle tap on his shoulder and told him he could get dressed. When Jack stood up, he smiled sheepishly at the three of us. "Thank you, thank you," he said. "I never thought I'd have the courage to ask a woman to fuck me." I guess I must have looked appalled by what I had just seen, because he turned to me and said, "You look as if you need to lie down."

He was probably right. The experience was so intense and surreal, I was reeling. How would I ever explain this experience to my husband? I thanked Jack for allowing me to watch and excused myself, leaving the three of them to chat about his life in Los Angeles. No one saw me leave Farrah's room, and I sneaked back into the parlor. I tried to act nonchalant and normal with the other women, but it was a struggle. What I had witnessed was like seeing a human being splayed out on a bed

with his guts exposed. It would take some time for me to as-
similate the whole experience.

News that Baby had let me watch one of her parties spread
in no time among the women. Somehow, luckily, staff and management managed to stay in the dark. Although some of the
women thought Baby had been reckless—management might
have caught her—others were fascinated. What did I think?
Did it arouse me? Did it disgust me? When Donna heard that I
had seen a dominance party, she squealed in horror. She had
been mortified the time she walked into Baby's room and saw
a client hog-tied to her shower head with one dildo in his anus
and one in his mouth. Donna refused to perform fantasy sessions, preferring instead straight, simple intercourse. Even in
her personal life, she was sexually conservative, and wouldn't
perform blow jobs on her husband. For the next several
weeks, whenever Donna and I passed each other, she blushed
and smiled uneasily.

Brittany had an entirely different reaction. When she
learned that I had watched one of Baby's parties, she seemed
crestfallen. I saw in her face hurt and disappointment. "I
would've let you watch one of *my* parties," she said. Over the
last several weeks, I had been aware of a strange competitive
tension developing between her and Baby for my attention.

Brittany tried to hide her competitive feelings behind criticism: "Baby and Farrah should have paid you something. You
should have made some money, because the customer liked
you being there. They could have negotiated for more." Jack
had paid $500, the women splitting their cut 50–50. I told her
that I wouldn't have dreamed of accepting money and that

Baby had done me a favor. She had shown me what happened in the bedroom during paid sex so I could better understand the work of a prostitute.

But Brittany wouldn't hear it. If Baby had really wanted me to appreciate her work, Brittany argued, then she wouldn't have had me watch a dominance party. Dominance was easy for prostitutes, she said. It was a release to get to beat a customer and be verbally cruel, all for pay. Far harder, she said, was faking intimacy, acting lustful and passionate with every customer.

Brittany didn't drop the subject. The next weekend, when Norman, one of her regular customers, came in, she made a point of introducing him to me. After a brief exchange, I stood up to leave them in privacy; Norman said he hadn't seen Brittany for several weeks. But Brittany asked me to stay, saying that Norman didn't mind. Her eyes fixed on mine with steely insistence. The next thing I knew, she was ordering drinks for us both, compliments of Norman.

Norman was a heavyset man in his mid-fifties with Coke-bottle glasses. Whenever he spoke, his eyelids fluttered closed. He spoke very slowly and haltingly, as if constantly struggling for the right words. He looked like a big sheepdog, with a sheep's obedient, passive nature. Brittany later told me that she had been seeing Norman for over a year, since soon after her move to Mustang Ranch from neighboring Old Bridge Ranch, where she had worked for several years. Devastated by the retirement of the prostitute he previously frequented, Norman had quickly become one of Brittany's regulars, visiting her nearly every month. Never married and still living at home with his mother, he had seen a succession of brothel prostitutes since his first visit to Nevada's brothels many years earlier with his father, since deceased.

After we had chatted at the bar for about thirty minutes, Norman became noticeably restless and obviously ready to go to Brittany's room. She led him away. In about five minutes, she returned in a silk bathrobe, alone, to book Norman's money with the cashier. On the way back to her room, she called me over to the hallway leading down to her bedroom. She had asked Norman if I could watch them "make love," she told me, and, ever accommodating, he had agreed.

I was taken aback. This awkward, bumbling man was willing to let me watch him have sex? I was flabbergasted, and quite ambivalent. My experience with Baby and the architect had been so intense, I wasn't at all sure I was up to watching again. But if I really wanted to understand this place, how could I turn down the opportunity? Blanche was working as floor maid that night instead of Shelley, and I had little fear of getting caught. I gave Brittany a smile of assent and followed her down the hallway.

Before we arrived at her room, Brittany told me that Norman knew to tip me and that I should accept. When I tried to explain that I didn't want his money, she pooh-poohed me.

As she opened the door, I saw Norman lying naked on the bed like a beached whale. With his glasses off, he looked disoriented and confused. I couldn't fathom how Brittany could ever pretend to be attracted to this man. She was right: this had to be the hardest job of all. Brittany instructed me to make myself comfortable on a nearby chair, where Norman's royal blue golf shirt and matching polyester pants lay neatly folded. After dimming the overhead lights to a warm glow, she removed her robe while Norman gazed spellbound at her fleshy body. Brittany slinked over to where Norman lay supine, the top of his head grazing the headboard. She had already checked and washed his genitals, and she only had to put on the condom.

I watched as Brittany put a condom in her mouth before kneeling down on the bed to place it on the head of Norman's semi-erect penis. She began sucking slowly, concentrating on rolling down the rubber with her mouth, careful not to tear it with her teeth. Brittany could take Norman's entire penis in her mouth, and this enabled her to push the rim of the condom down to the base with her lips. Simultaneously, her left hand stroked and gently manipulated his engorged testes to further arouse him. "Oh, Norman, you are so big, so beautiful," she murmured intermittently.

In one awkward moment, Brittany stopped sucking and slipped out of her role to offer me a pointer on condoms. "One of the fallacies is that you shouldn't put a condom on when the penis isn't hard. But we do that all the time without a problem. You just have to remember to hold on to it until the penis gets more erect," she instructed with the conscientiousness of my junior high English teacher. I felt self-conscious and terribly out of place, afraid my presence was distracting her from her work, ruining the experience for Norman, and putting her job in jeopardy. But when I glanced over at Norman, who lay silent and immobile, defenseless and delirious under her touch, I realized he hadn't even noticed the pause.

Brittany continued to give Norman oral sex for several more minutes before lifting her head. Then, moving together synchronously like longtime dance partners, the twosome changed positions in silence, with Brittany ending up on her back and Norman prepared to enter her. At this point, Brittany caught my eye and told me to move closer. Obediently I pulled my chair alongside the bed, although I had the distinct sensation of being too close, as if in the first row of a movie theater. I watched as Brittany wrapped her legs around Norman's broad body to draw him deeper as he thrust his pelvis against her. His grunts encouraged her to whisper provocatively, "Oh, Norman. You make me so wet. You're such a man." She knew exactly what he needed to feel virile. She glanced over at me once or twice to make sure I was watching.

Brittany turned her attention back to Norman and urged him on with sweet talk in between nibbles on his ear. He thrust for about five minutes, then rolled off her with a sigh, a look of defeat darkening his face. Brittany patted him consolingly on his chest. "Gee, you haven't been in to see me for some time. Don't worry, you'll come." Norman frequently had trouble. I said I hoped it wasn't my intrusive presence that had made orgasm difficult for him, to which Brittany responded emphatically, "It wasn't you. He just has trouble sometimes. He gets too excited—don't you, Norman?" The backup plan for Norman was to take him to the Jacuzzi to relax him a bit before returning to try again. The second attempt usually resulted in success.

Brittany used this break to go to the bathroom, leaving me alone, face-to-face, with her naked customer. I asked if he was sure he didn't mind my being there. I suspected that he would never admit it in front of Brittany. "Whatever Brittany wants," said Norman. "It seemed really important to her to let you watch, so I said it was okay. I only want to make her happy. My only reason for coming here is to give Brittany pleasure." To give Brittany *pleasure*? I kept a straight face, but I did wonder how a brothel customer could ever allow himself to think that that was what this was all about.

At this point, Norman stood up and reached for his pants. "I'd like to tip you," he said. Brittany had put him up to this. For the briefest of seconds, I thought to myself how easy it would be to take this gullible man's money. Like the women said, A trick is to be tricked. But I just couldn't bring myself to accept. It felt too exploitative, especially in light of the fact this man was smitten with Brittany and willing to do almost anything she asked. What would it have said about me to take advantage of his vulnerability? I thanked him for the offer but told him not to worry about it. Seeming relieved, he quickly slid his wallet back into his pants pocket.

As soon as Brittany emerged from the toilet, I thanked them both and quickly excused myself. I breathed a huge sigh of relief as I walked back to the parlor. I'd felt more uncomfortable watching Brittany than I had watching Baby. Brittany's time with Norman felt profoundly more intimate than Baby's party with the architect, in which I had felt like an on-looker at a circus sideshow. With Norman and Brittany I was an intruder.

As soon as Norman left, Brittany tracked me down to make sure he had paid me. At first I lied, so as not to upset her. Then she asked me how much—he had told her $40—and I realized I was just going to get caught. She didn't really think I had accepted Norman's money. I admitted that while he had offered a tip, I hadn't accepted it. I asked her not to be angry with Norman; he was only trying to make her happy.

In fact, she was furious with *me*. It was weak and foolish of me to want to protect Norman. Didn't I understand that I was working against her, not with her, when I refused his money? Taking his money wasn't exploitative but rather fair trade, she said, a service in kind, an arrangement established long ago between the first prostitute and her customer. To turn down Norman's money was paramount to telling him that payment wasn't always necessary. Prostitution worked solely on the assumption that men paid for a woman's services—her time, personal attention, or sexual prowess—all of which were valuable. A customer's payment acknowledged the pains the prostitute took to meet his needs. Taking money from Norman was important, Brittany explained, softening some now, so he wouldn't forget he was just a customer.

I started to understand her point. While a good prostitute was able to get a man to forget he was a paying customer dur-ing sex, afterward he needed to remember it was merely a business exchange and not mistake it for a real relationship. But sometimes the women were too good at what they did, and the men came to believe in the fantasies they were paying for—like Norman, who started to believe in Brittany's illusion of intimacy and to feel that he was special. Whenever this happened—whenever a man forgot he was a customer—the prostitute's relationship with him grew complicated.

5 .. ENTANGLEMENTS

One day Baby showed me a letter written on four pages of standard 8½-x-11-inch paper carefully torn along the perforated edge of a notebook. It was from one of her regulars, who, upon reflection at the time of his forty-first birthday, wanted to thank Baby for all she had done. In it, he said: *"With you for my sweet and special friend, I don't feel like I'm alone in this world, it makes me feel wonderful and alive that you are the beautiful lady in my life."* He closed the letter pledging to serve her every wish.

It was a Sunday morning postshift, and Baby had invited me down into her room. The letter was the latest in a string she had received from Philip, a local man who had been coming to Mustang Ranch to see her for seven years.

Baby was used to having admirers, customers who

showered her with cards and gifts ranging from flowers and perfume to jewelry and lingerie. These love tokens either arrived by mail or were brought in person whenever her regulars came to town. But Philip was probably Baby's most devoted customer. True to his word, he catered to her every whim; it wasn't unusual for him to run several errands a week for her, such as taking her compact disc player in for repair, or buying a card for her to send to her mom on Mother's Day.

One weekend morning, Philip, a slight man with a dark, thick mustache, showed up at Mustang #1 at nine A.M. to help Roberto, the Mustang handyman, sand and stain pieces of redwood to use as bedposts for Baby's room. Philip had bought the wood at a lumber store. Because of her seniority, Baby didn't have to pack up her room when she left the brothel on vacation but was allowed to keep it intact, with the understanding that another woman would probably be assigned there temporarily in her absence. This privilege brought with it the freedom to personalize her room any way she wanted. When Baby expressed a desire to redecorate, Philip offered to foot the bill.

According to Baby, Philip epitomized the man who came out to the brothels looking for someone to fall in love with. He had met Baby at a particularly vulnerable time in his life. An alcoholic, he had hit rock bottom after his second drunk-driving charge, and he had shown up at Mustang Ranch in despair, desperate for a friend. For a fee of $300, Baby became the person he could, in his words, "reach out and grasp onto." That first night, he promised her he would quit drinking. Indeed, he had maintained his sobriety since, and he credited

Baby with his transformation. "She brings out the best in me," Philip would later tell me. "If it hadn't been for Baby, I would have eventually been in prison or died. That's why I like doing things for her, like bringing her gifts and doing her favors."

Baby wasn't surprised at Philip's infatuation. "We prostitutes are paid to be the perfect partners. We're agreeable to whatever the customer says or feels about life. Because we're so understanding and supportive, sometimes the clients fall in love with us." What Baby described didn't sound that different from a patient finding unconditional acceptance from a therapist (also for a handsome fee) and mistaking their feelings of appreciation for feelings of love. Real relationships weren't nearly as easy and demanded more compromises. It was no wonder that everyone else in Philip's life disappointed him. In no time, Philip became one of Baby's regulars.

Most Mustang prostitutes had a collection of regulars who visited them habitually and exclusively. Regular customers were the bread and butter of the business, enabling the women to get through the slow seasons when tourism tapered off. Baby was particularly talented at fostering regulars. Even the selection of her working name had been intentional. "I picked it so I would always be in their heads," she said. "When they're at home making love to their wives or girlfriends and say, 'Ooh, Baby!' they have to think of me at the same time." Her results spoke for themselves. Baby serviced between seventy and eighty customers per week and she generated $300,000 worth of revenue for the brothel for seven months of work; her take of it was close to $150,000.

But regulars were as varied in their fantasies as the rest of the brothel clientele. Baby knew that in order to sustain regular customers like Philip—men who wanted intimacy and the feeling of being special—she had to give them the illusion of mutuality. To that end, she gave Philip her pager number and her supposed real name and details about her outside life, to make it seem as if she had begun letting down her guard. According to Baby, the effect on Philip had been striking. Very quickly, he began visiting every week rather than just a few times a month. Believing Baby's increased openness meant he was more than simply a customer, Philip started acting bolder in the bedroom and more confident in the parlor. Baby had taken pride in his development.

More recently, however, things had become difficult. Philip was coming out to Mustang ever more often, several times a week. He showed up promptly at nine P.M. on Friday and Saturday nights in the hopes of being Baby's first customer of the evening. At first, Baby had found this level of devotion endearing, a flattering acknowledgment of the quality of her work. Over time, however, she found herself growing annoyed. "I don't want him to be my first party every weekend," she said. "I get excited dressing up and thinking about hitting the floor, and then there he is. It's a drag to start a shift with Philip."

Philip had no idea of the annoyance he was causing Baby. He thought he was her salvation each night. Baby sent over other women to hustle Philip in the hope that he might lose his intense interest in her, but he refused them, announcing loudly that he wouldn't dream of hurting Baby's feelings by being with anyone else.

I first laid eyes on Philip one night as Baby walked him

back to the parlor after his usual thirty minutes of cuddling and a half and half. I noticed that he loitered around the bar for several hours, trying to catch glimpses of Baby between customers. He followed her every move intently, once scowling when Baby flirtatiously raked her long, manicured fingernails across another man's chest. When Baby spotted him staring, she didn't even bother to act polite. No, she didn't want a drink, she said coldly, and yes, she was still busy working. Despite raising her voice and sharpening her tone a number of times, Baby couldn't shake him. Philip didn't leave the brothel until almost four A.M.

Recently, Philip had decided that he wanted to be Baby's white knight and take her away from the brothel life. He promised he would take care of her financially. Baby rejected his offers brusquely. He had become irritating, and she put too high a premium on her freedom. "I feel like I'm choking," she told me later. Besides, she figured she earned more money working at Mustang than she could ever get out of Philip. But he was nothing if not persistent; I saw him waiting on Baby whenever I visited Mustang.

Sugar daddies—smitten men who offered women financial help if they would quit the business—were usually highly sought-after commodities. Women spent countless hours recounting tales of the various spoils they had obtained from their sugar daddies. One brothel worker told a wealthy Arizona rancher she would need $14,000 for her son to get a much needed ear operation and $100,000 to open her own business. In exchange, it was understood—either explicitly or implicitly—that the prostitute would become the man's girlfriend. For the woman, such an arrangement was merely business, not significantly different from prostituting in a brothel except that she had only one customer to deal with. The woman would keep secret her true feelings, as she would the existence of a boyfriend or husband.

Keri, the woman who had been with the mentally troubled virgin, was a good example. Several years earlier, she told me, she had managed to turn a $60 date (Mustang's minimum at the time) into a sugar daddy. In the course of four and a half years, she got this man to spend thousands of dollars on her, for her own apartment, clothing, jewelry, cosmetic surgery, and a car. "He came at the perfect time," she said. "I was tired of the business. I wanted to be at home with my daughter. So I just came up with the story that I was sad because I wasn't making any money and I missed my daughter. When he heard this, he said he wanted to provide for me and to take care of my daughter. He said he would marry me."

Incredibly, Keri managed never to have sex with this man. "When I met him at Mustang, I only gave him hand jobs and he felt my boobs. When I left the brothel to be with him, I told him I wanted to wait to have sex until we got married." Perhaps even more incredibly, he believed her. Things finally ended, however, the way they do with most sugar daddies: he found out that she had two children and was pregnant with her third. Hit in the face with reality, he called the relationship off.

All the women expected their relationships with sugar daddies to come to an end eventually. Sometimes they ended when the men became too emotionally attached and too demanding, and sometimes simply because the men went broke. I heard countless examples of men who went into bankruptcy trying to maintain their kept women. Only rarely would a woman stay long term with a sugar daddy, and then it was usually for security's sake and not for love.

Sometimes, though, it was the prostitute who complicated the professional relationship. Like a prostitute named Mercedes had done with a customer named Gary. Gary had been Mercedes's regular for over two years. In his early thirties, with curly brown shoulder-length hair, a soft gentle voice, and acne scars across his face, Gary was a self-professed late bloomer who was very shy with girls. He first visited Mustang, in his words, "out of desperation." Although he wasn't a virgin, he had limited sexual experience. Gary picked Mercedes, a tall, slender African-American woman in her mid-thirties, out of a lineup because of his attraction to black women. When she provided his most exciting and confidence-building sexual encounter yet, he got hooked. To her surprise, so did she.

Whenever Mercedes flew back to Reno from her home out of state, she called up Gary and begged him to come out to Mustang to keep her company. For reasons I didn't entirely understand, at one point she began giving Gary a portion of her earnings. Gary once explained to me: "One night she said, 'There's nothing like giving the money you make to a man.' When I told her I didn't want her money, she started to cry. When I finally agreed, she asked me what my quota was. I didn't know what to say except that she should figure it out.

The next day, a cabdriver came to my place and handed me a manila envelope from Mercedes with nine hundred dollars in it."

To Gary, Mercedes was a little girl who needed taking care of, and turning him into a pimp was her way of communicating that she had chosen him to be her protector. Flattered that this prostitute was opening herself up to him, Gary soon developed a serious crush on his ward. Mercedes continued to give him money for a couple of months, until one day when she abruptly cut him off. "She told me she could give it to me as fast as she could take it away," said Gary. "It was because I had lost my job and was beginning to get coddled by her. As soon as she saw me as weak, she got mean. Now she wants the money back that she gave me. I'm a failed apprentice."

According to Gary, Mercedes had an older man at home, an attorney, whom she considered her boyfriend, someone who took care of her, he speculated, "like it was his job because she's so lost emotionally." Had Mercedes chosen Gary to fill in while she was away from home? Surely she had learned over the years what effective tools money and sex are. Or had her years at streetwalking habituated her to bestowing her hard-earned money on a man in order to feel valuable and worthy? Gary wasn't sure what role he served for Mercedes. He wasn't even convinced that the emotions Mercedes expressed with him were completely genuine. He thought she had been a prostitute too long and had learned to sequester her emotions so well that she was unable to feel anything with her customers.

Like Philip, Gary didn't know how the woman with whom he was infatuated really felt about him. This was a hazard of becoming entangled with a working girl. But it didn't seem to matter all that much. Regardless of Mercedes's true motives, Gary cherished the fact that she had opened up to him at all. He felt special. "I've resigned myself to be her little friend in Reno. Sometimes she says she loves me and other times she says I'm her boy toy. I'll be whatever she wants and needs me to be for her. I only hope she gets some pleasure from me."

Pleasure. That was the question that had been on my mind since I'd first arrived in Nevada: Did any of the working girls enjoy the sex? Gary, Philip, and Norman each imagined sharing a mutually satisfying emotional connection with their favorite prostitutes, and so naturally they hoped or assumed that the women enjoyed the sex too. But Baby and Brittany explicitly told me they didn't enjoy sex with Philip and Norman. Were prostitutes ever sexually satisfied by their customers, or were they always physically shut down during paid sex, as Brittany had told her husband at dinner?

One morning a few weeks later, I had gotten up early and found the night working girls still busy. Some lay curled up on parlor couches napping, while others escorted freshly shaven men back to their rooms for morning pre-work quickies. I always wondered about these early birds—did they wake up burning with lust, or was this stress prophylaxis before a big day?

I spotted Carrie, the woman whose mother pimped her, emerging from her room with her customer, a huge smirk

across her face, used towels in hand. As she led him back to
the front entrance, she winked at one of the other girls who
had been dozing on the couch. She steered the young black
man, dressed from head to toe in FUBU hip-hop gear, over to a
coffee table to give him a book of Mustang matches as a souvenir and to give her friend a better view. At the doorway, she
grazed the young man's arm and stretched up to whisper in his
ear. He pecked her lightly on the nose before turning to go.

Carrie walked back into the parlor with a silly grin still
plastered across her face. Her cherry-red lipstick looked
smudged, as if she had been kissing, though house rules prohibited it. The spot of lipstick his peck had planted on the tip
of her nose confirmed it.

"Did you put your money in, too?" teased one of the girls
from the couch.

"No," said Carrie in a serious tone. "But he was so fine.
He had such a nice body." She moved her hands as if to out-
line his broad shoulders and strapping chest. "And when he
took off his baseball hat—oo-ee!" She turned on her heels and
with a slight wiggle of her hips strode back to her room to
clean up.

The playful teasing of the other women contrasted sharply
with the abuse heaped on a prostitute named Stacy a few days
later when she announced to the parlor how tired she was after being with seven customers and having an orgasm with
each one. I had stumbled upon a never-ending debate: Should
a prostitute permit herself to enjoy sex with her customers? As
I came to learn how divided the prostitutes were on this issue,

I started bringing it up casually at mealtimes and saw how quickly emotions stirred and tempers flared.

"I'm numb back there with customers," a prostitute named Linda said with conviction one night over crab legs. "There's nothing a man here could do to turn me on." The two other women at the table nodded their heads in agreement. The three had worked together at Mustang for over a decade.

"Working girls should *never* enjoy sex with a customer," Linda added. "You save that for your man." She spoke so loudly and with such authority that several of the women at neighboring tables stopped talking to look up. One of Baby's friends sitting alone at another table stiffened her spine. Linda either didn't notice or didn't care.

Then one of the women sitting next to Linda explained how her man had taught her this principle when she first turned out. Her then-pimp spent almost two months preparing her. "He watched me have sex with his friends to teach me the dos and don'ts. You know, not to let him stroke me too long or fuck me too hard. He stood right there and watched to make sure I didn't let the guy put his fingers inside me, that I maintained complete control of the situation and didn't get aroused." Such practices weren't uncommon, Linda added.

Linda's man had turned her out in a massage parlor in the Midwest almost twenty years ago. Now in her early forties, Linda tended to attract older men, many of them widowed or divorced, who sought companionship and affection even more than sex. A blonde with teased shoulder-length hair and spiked bangs, she usually wore leotards with short-waisted jackets or belts to distract the eye from her middle-age spread. Although she wasn't the most beautiful woman in the house, she had a very sympathetic face and a demeanor that made her customers feel safe.

She had learned to disassociate quickly after her first couple of dates as a new turn-out, she said. "It's like putting up a block in your mind. You go through the motions, but you're not really there, you're taking a trip out of the room. I put myself on a sandy beach somewhere. Or, I think about something I really want to do, say plant those shrubs and do a garden when I get home. Or, I think about the money. The calculator is always *cha-ching-ing* while the guy's fucking me." I imagined how deflated any of her regulars would be if they could hear her *cha-ching-ing*.

"Why would I want to enjoy sex with just anybody that walked in off the street?" Linda said. "That's like a one-night stand. I've never been that type of person. I have to be comfortable with the person. There's got to be more to it for me to enjoy sex with him."

I almost literally had to bite my tongue. Linda had never been a person who was comfortable having one-night stands? What did she sell daily? Weren't one-night stands with countless anonymous men the prostitute's job description exactly? She didn't see it this way. Professional sex was work, and very different for her from personal sex.

"To enjoy sex with a customer is to lower yourself to his level," Linda added. Her remark exemplified the fundamental disrespect that—despite the pride they took in their work—

almost all prostitutes had for their customers. But Linda's low opinion of johns did not preclude pride in her work or the ambition of pleasing her customers; what it did was enable her to be an ever-accommodating chameleon for all her customers in a controlled, contained, deliberate way, all the while justifiably compartmentalizing her experience and keeping her emotional world inaccessible to these men.

"I think women who enjoy sex with customers are fooling themselves, looking for love in the wrong place," said Linda. "They can't find a man on the outside so they get some in here." At that, Baby's friend at the next table abruptly rose and stormed out of the kitchen. Linda and her friends pretended not to notice.

No one spoke up that night to contradict Linda, but a few days later, Baby and the woman who had stormed out of the room approached me. "We just want you to know that some women see nothing wrong with enjoying sex with their customers," Baby said. "It just depends on the customer."

The other woman added, "Linda and those other women were lying. With as much sex as we have, how could a woman not enjoy it occasionally?"

Still, they explained, most women who did enjoy sex with their clients didn't speak openly about it in the brothel for fear of stigmatization and of upsetting their partners at home. Baby said she had no shame admitting it to her peers, but there were consequences. She had to put up with cruel gossip and derisive remarks: "Baby freaks for her customers"; "Baby loves to get nasty with her tricks."

Instead of denigrating the women who refused to enjoy

sex with customers, Baby said she felt sorry for them. "I try to make my sex life good anytime I'm having sex. If you're gonna have sex with strangers, your best bet is to try to make the most of the situation, you know. Honestly, I think some of the most uptight, sexually frustrated, sexually repressed women I've ever met work in whorehouses."

After a little more inquiry, though, I found that sexual arousal occurred more frequently than not. In fact, over three-quarters of the women confessed to me in private that they had experienced sexual excitement with clients, and a full 70 percent admitted to having had an orgasm with a customer. Ten percent of the women confided that they orgasmed *more often* with clients than they did with lovers, and 8 percent said they did just as frequently.

The reality, of course, was that women could and did enjoy sex with their customers despite pressure from their peers not to. Concealment perpetuated the stigma. That this of all professions would have a code of propriety that stigmatized enjoying sex with customers struck me as ironic.

Much more taboo was actually falling in love with a customer. This was viewed by women like Linda as not only unprofessional but self-destructive. Veteran prostitutes believed that working girls in love with johns were doomed because the relationships could amount to only one thing: pain. Although all was usually well at the outset, as soon as the couple began having disagreements the man would inevitably tell the woman she was nothing but a whore. "He makes it clear that he's done you a favor by getting you out of there," said Linda.

"And that you can't do nothing without him but go back and be a whore." Too frequently, this power imbalance destroyed the relationship; the woman returned to the brothel, humbled by having trusted a trick.

According to Linda, customers were a different caliber of man than any she would consider marrying. Customers had to pay for "it" and were apparently incapable of getting their needs satisfied without offering women money. "Once a man walks through the door, he's a trick," said Linda. "That's all he's ever going to be. I wouldn't have any respect for him, because he's buying sex. I couldn't look at him without that crossing my mind." And what was to say he wouldn't pay for it again? As the brothel adage went, "Once a trick, always a trick." Day in and day out, brothel prostitutes depended on adulterous men to earn a living, but like the rest of us, none wanted to be on the other side, to be the betrayed lover.

Despite these arguments, I often heard George and other brothel owners recount tales of women who met their Prince Charming in the brothels. These stories were typically told to show that brothels offered women opportunity, including the chance to fall in love.

During my time at the brothels, I witnessed one such case myself. Alice was a new turn-out, a forty-seven-year-old recent divorcée who hadn't prostituted a day in her life. And you could tell. Dressed in sheer silk blouses with a camisole underneath, tailored slacks and skirts, and a string of pearls, she looked as if she belonged at a country club. She'd come to Mustang Ranch after watching a special on the brothel on an evening news show. Her husband had just left her for a younger woman, but not before cleaning out their checking and savings accounts, and she needed to provide for herself and her developmentally disabled teenage daughter.

With the elegance of a retired Southern beauty pageant winner and the fresh, naïve look of a new turn-out, which always seemed to appeal to Mustang customers, Alice was picked frequently. She said she got through her first trick—a sweaty trucker who refused her offer of a shower—by closing her eyes and envisioning her daughter's face.

It was in her first days at Mustang that she met Bruce, a divorced fifty-year-old ex-cop who had recently moved to Nevada. Bruce had been celibate for over nine months, channeling all his energy into a new business. It was his woman-chasing business associate who dragged him out to Mustang, where Bruce only intended to grab a beer to be able to say he had visited the famous brothel. But when Alice joined him at the bar, he found himself smitten. They talked at length, and after Bruce and his friend left, Bruce found himself unable to get Alice out of his mind. Impressed by her sophistication and refinement, he decided to turn around and drive back to Mustang. "I just couldn't believe the words she was talking," explained Bruce. "She wasn't trashy."

Back at the brothel, he followed Alice directly to her room. In fact, Bruce drove out to Mustang every night for a week to follow Alice to her room. It was only a matter of days before he fell in love and started fantasizing about being with her long-term. "I've never felt this way before, and it isn't because

I was taking her to bed. I could come out here, sit in her room for two hours, and just talk to her. She's an intelligent lady, and I would love to be with her all the time." Many customers admitted to me that they had similar short-lived fantasies but most talked themselves out of it. Bruce's friend tried to do the convincing for him, thinking Bruce had lost his grip on reality, was spending money recklessly, and was probably being duped.

But Alice had also begun falling for Bruce. As they talked more and more, she found herself fantasizing about being taken care of and loved by this man. "There was something very special about him. He was very, very sensitive about my needs. He didn't ask the usual questions, like, Why is a girl like you here in a place like this? I loved that." In short, Bruce treated Alice like a normal woman. She didn't need to be ashamed at having resorted to prostitution. She even let herself begin envisioning rebuilding a life with Bruce not unlike the one she'd lost—a stable life with a decent man by her side.

Although the other girls told her never to trust a trick, Alice found herself unable to stop. Bruce seemed different from the other customers, she told herself. Just to be certain, she asked him if he would ever use her work to pass judgment against her. His response: "I don't care what's happened in the past. Once you walk out of here, that's the past. I will never hold it against you." While Alice found reassurance in his words, some of the skeptical veterans confided to me that Bruce's answer was classic, no different from that of other men who dreamed a relationship with a prostitute might work out.

The two began making wedding plans. Meanwhile, Alice continued to prostitute, hoping to pull herself out of her financial crisis. Bruce came out every night after work. Now friendly with Mustang's staff, he sat at the bar while Alice saw johns. As long as she stayed in the brothel and took up space, the house expected Alice to continue earning money, and Bruce continued having to pay to go back to her room if he wanted time alone with her. Bruce compared the situation to conjugal visits in prison. He admitted feeling uncomfortable watching other men take his future bride back to the bedroom. But it was only a matter of weeks before Alice finally gave up her job, telling me she could no longer have sex with other men knowing Bruce was outside waiting.

I stayed in touch with Alice. For several years, she and Bruce remained together. But then, as Linda and others had predicted, in the middle of a heated argument the past resurfaced: despite Bruce's original good intentions, he reminded Alice where he had found her. Several weeks later, the couple broke up. Alice managed to defy Linda's stereotype and never returned to her brothel career. She quickly married another man who knew nothing about her past. "Our hobbies include tennis, golf, and cocktail hours," she wrote to me of her new life in one holiday letter. It sounded as if her new husband would have had an aneurysm had he known about her brief career.

Few women working at Mustang were willing to admit falling for customers. Over time, as they got to know me, more did begin to confess—but in strict confidence. One night, Brittany revealed that Jon, her husband, was a former trick. Like

Linda, Brittany had been trained by her pimp not to trust her tricks. "I learned early on not to cross that professional boundary," she said. "It's like violating the doctor-patient line." But when she met Jon, she fell in love in spite of herself and everything she had learned.

Three and a half years earlier, Jon had paid his first visit to the Reno brothels. He was with a group of friends. "I fell in love when I turned around and saw her the first time," he said. "I didn't want her sexually or anything. I just felt a warm attraction to her." Brittany admitted she had felt something similar and found herself surprisingly excited when Jon and his friends decided to take her and a few other working girls on an outdate ($1,000 per woman). Jon said he and his friends proposed this just so Jon and Brittany could be together outside the brothel.

In town, they went dancing and gambling in the casinos before heading to the hotel bedrooms. Although Brittany and Jon fooled around, Jon couldn't have intercourse. "I didn't want vaginal sex because I knew I felt something for her. I didn't know what at the time. I just wanted to talk to her." At the end of the night, Brittany shocked herself when she gave him a peck on the lips, something she had never before done with a customer. "It just seemed so natural," she recalled. "Like we already knew each other."

After silencing the voices of doubt in her head, Brittany decided to take the initiative and call Jon in his Reno hotel before he drove back home to Santa Rosa. "I knew if he ever called me at the Ranch, he would become fixed as a trick in my mind. I had to call him to establish a connection outside the brothel." Because of Jon's fear that Brittany was simply out to develop business on the side, she had to tell him directly that she had no interest in a professional relationship.

Slowly, the couple began dating long distance, with frequent telephone calls and trips back and forth between Reno and Santa Rosa. Although both had their doubts about pursuing the relationship, Brittany was the one to become insecure, to lose all the sexual confidence she had gained as a prostitute. "I didn't know how to handle the sex part. All of a sudden I'm totally naïve, like a teenager who doesn't know how to have sex." It was Jon who took the lead and gently guided the couple's physical relationship.

Six months later, Brittany and Jon moved in. They lived together for a year and a half before deciding to marry. Even after three years of marriage, Brittany remained cautious, anticipating the day Jon might become like all the other horror-story tricks and tell her she was nothing but a whore. Meanwhile, Jon feared that Brittany might fall in love with another customer.

I understood why Brittany kept this secret from her peers, especially after seeing how judgmental Linda and the others could be. But I would realize later that the women's harshness about dating tricks only hinted at how catty and vicious the women could really be.

6 .. SISTERHOOD

Around noon one day a new woman named Heather approached me while I was eating lunch in the kitchen at Mustang #1. At first, she pretended to be making casual conversation, but she was clearly unnerved. She asked how my day was going, and before I could answer, she said, "*I've* sure had one hell of a morning."

She sniffed and winced. "I was taking a shower. I reached for my shampoo. It had a strange odor, it smelled like perfume mixed with rotten eggs. Fumes filled up my nose and the back of my throat. The shower steamed up, and I felt almost claustrophobic. Then my scalp began to tingle, then burn. That's when I knew. Someone had put Nair in my shampoo."

Heather had been a victim of terrorism brothel-style, an attempt by colleagues to intimidate her, perhaps even chase her out, as they did frequently to new girls who threatened their business.

As she spoke, her body language—stooped shoulders, nervous hands, pain-lined face—spoke of her need for reassurance. Like other new arrivals at Mustang Ranch, she had no allies in place to protect or defend her. I wondered if she realized how little influence I, an outsider, had.

Heather and I had gotten acquainted a week earlier, as we found ourselves headed through the brothel gate together for a jog one morning. We were almost the only women who left the compound to exercise—the brothel strongly discouraged it and ordered us to stay on Mustang property—and we agreed to become running mates. During our runs, we talked, and I came to know her well.

This was Heather's first trip to one of Nevada's legal brothels. For more than four years, she had worked full-time in illegal brothels in Houston's business district, until a recent crackdown by the city's vice squad forced her to temporarily relocate out of state. Previous professional success had made her quite confident. "I'm big-time in Houston. I make easy money," she told me on one run. "I didn't think it would be like that here too, but it is." She snickered.

Still, the move to Reno had been daunting. "I was really scared when I came to Mustang," she said. "I knew what it would be like when I got here. I knew what the prostitute life was about—competing. You know nobody's going to like you. You know it'll be really cold and unfriendly."

As Heather had anticipated, her reception at Mustang had

been chilly. Her arrival, in May, coincided with an unusual lull in business; sometimes three or four hours passed before a customer rang the doorbell. Meanwhile, Mustang #1 was nearly filled with women, with almost fifty ready to work each day of the typically busy season. With wigs and makeup in place, dressed in tight-fitting bodysuits and dresses, women sprawled on parlor couches, fretted about their financial obligations, and bickered relentlessly. Tension mounted, resentment boiled, hostility permeated the brothel. This was no time for the likes of Heather.

A chestnut-haired Bridget Fonda look-alike, Heather was a muscularly built woman with a provocative smile that revealed a small gap between her two front teeth. Her work attire alternated between two identical blue and pink skintight polka-dot dresses with teardrop-shaped cutouts to expose her firm midriff. Her looks didn't go unnoticed; it wasn't unusual for her to be chosen from lineup five out of six times.

From the beginning, she had experienced animosity from her colleagues. "The first day I came out to the parlor wearing a little white dress, high heels, and makeup, they said in snotty tones, 'Oh, you look different.' I knew what they meant. I'd heard it before. They were thinking, 'Uh-oh, she's pretty. She's going to get picked over us.' They don't like me very much. In a way, I guess it's a compliment. Then, in another way, it kind of gets on my nerves. I'm friendly, and I like other people to be friendly to me." Behind Heather's almost bratty defensiveness, I sensed true hurt feelings.

The other women constantly exchanged catty remarks

about Heather, usually when she was within earshot. "She just thinks she's so beautiful." "Aren't you ready to go to bed yet?" "Why don't you take that dress off?" "Aren't you tired of fucking yet?" One woman told customers that Heather was a lesbian and hated men.

Strain between Heather and her colleagues culminated in the Nair incident. "I was pissed, I mean *pissed*. I went straight to Keri, my bathmate. I was like, 'Keri, I don't know if I'm crazy or not.' I let her smell it. She said, 'No, girl. That's something nasty. That's Nair, bleach, or something.' I stormed into the parlor with my shampoo bottle in hand. I looked pissed, and some of the girls were like, 'What's wrong with you?' I said, 'Somebody put fucking Nair in my shampoo.' "

There was no doubt that the attack was aimed at Heather. "My hair products were in *my* room. We don't keep our stuff in the bathroom. At first, everybody wanted to accuse Keri, but she's like me. When she first came here years ago, somebody poked holes in her condoms. She warned me to lock up my condoms. But I didn't think about my shampoo. I just left it out."

Keri urged Heather to complain to the management. Despite their usual hands-off policy regarding feuding women, the managers were furious that the other women would threaten a worker who was making considerable money for the house when business was in such a slump. The visiting beautician, who happened to be at the brothel for her weekly house call, was paid to wash and condition Heather's hair using salon products and special pH treatments. Because all of Heather's shampoos and conditioners had been tampered with, she was given cash compensation. House rules required women to keep the doors to their rooms unlocked, but Heather was given a key and told to lock hers.

News of the attack spread quickly, the story being embellished as it was told and retold. Some women claimed the shampoo had been replaced with acid. Several believed that an older prostitute must have committed the act, because Nair was an ancient trick to run a prostitute out of a brothel. But Heather suspected a younger woman, someone directly losing business to her: "I'm not stealing the older girls' money. It's the other young brunettes whose business I'm hurting."

Long before Heather's Nair fiasco, I had wondered how the women really felt about one another. Competition was the name of the game at Mustang Ranch. During their twelve-hour shifts, women competed directly with each other. Unlike street prostitutes, they couldn't roam to solicit business on their own. Confined to the brothel, they had to wait for the doorbell to ring. By the time a client stepped into the parlor, women were lined up shoulder to shoulder to be scrutinized. If the client opted to go to the bar, the race was on to see who could hustle him into a room.

Not being picked could result in hurt feelings. Women frequently internalized rejection, blaming themselves for gaining weight, growing old, needing a boob job, or losing their ambition. And sometimes, other women like Heather were made to blame.

So it was no surprise that feuds and catfights were common. I had already seen numerous scuffles break out over borrowed clothing that was returned damaged, and loaned money that was never repaid. Until the Nair incident, though, I hadn't realized how deep the undercurrent of competition ran and how vindictive the women could be.

Irene, Mustang #2's manager, told me she warned all new women about the house pecking order. "It's hard when a girl first comes into a brothel. The girls who are already there are all of a sudden senior and the new girl becomes their target. If she does well, the ones who've been here awhile who aren't making any money, and are instead sitting back on the couches smoking cigarettes, get pissed at her. It's totally misdirected anger; their anger should be at themselves, at their own lack of interest and blasé attitude about the job. But the new girls who are enthusiastic and come in with a fresh attitude are always going to make more money simply because they're going to work harder."

Irene believed that management needed to intervene more frequently and more effectively. "It's about who's in control of the house. If you let all this stuff happen, you're going to keep your five or six clique-y girls, and they're going to chase everybody else out. You can't let that happen. You have to be aware that it's going on and nip it in the bud. You also have to talk to the new girls and tell them there's a possibility they're going to piss some people off, but that they're here to make money and need to keep their goals and objectives in mind."

Intimidation was nothing new to the brothels. Stories abounded about the old days, when women poured bleach on other women's clothing or threw blanket parties, in which a sleeping woman was covered in a blanket so she couldn't see who was beating her. More frequently, cattiness manifested itself in verbal attacks, name-calling (e.g., "slut"), bad-mouthing, physical fights, snitching, and ostracism. It wasn't unusual for brothel newcomers to quit under the pressure. Those who persevered earned their colleagues' grudging respect.

One day not long after the Nair shampoo incident, I wandered into the bar at Mustang #1 and caught several of the older women perched on bar stools, engrossed in a discussion about Heather, who had finally headed back to Houston for a weeklong vacation. "Not only was she cocky," said one of the women, "but did you see the way she tried to seduce the men in lineup?" According to these women, Heather had been targeted not because of jealousy over her popularity with customers but because she had been "dirty" hustling, drawing attention to herself at the expense of the other women. The other prostitutes considered dirty hustling the lowest of lows, a brothel crime. It merited serious retaliation, especially if committed during lineup, when women were expected to stand and speak their names demurely in accordance with long-established house rules. Heather was accused of batting her long lashes and mouthing her name seductively.

Over the course of my stay at Mustang, I often saw women overpromoting themselves or spoiling their co-workers' prospects with customers. How many times had I seen women call undue attention to themselves by rushing dramatically into lineup late or "accidentally" flashing their breasts and buttocks in the bar? A few women even rubbed men's crotches through their pants or whispered lewdly to them on the couches. Some women monopolized clients who showed no interest in them,

144 •• ALEXA ALBERT

simply to prevent their colleagues from snagging them. Still others intruded upon their peers while they were in the middle of a hustle.

It wasn't just that dirty hustling was an unethical, aggressive tactic, said many of the women. Dirty hustling could hurt everyone's business by offending and repelling customers. Equally reprehensible were those women who engaged in prohibited sex acts (e.g., kissing, anal sex, not using a condom) in order to snare a customer. When women broke these rules—which had been established primarily out of deference to the women's wishes—men stopped believing that they were ever in effect, and that undermined other prostitutes' ability to uphold them.

In an attempt to prevent dirty hustling, brothel management paired up all new working girls with more experienced prostitutes who were expected to teach newcomers the house's rules of etiquette, along with how to negotiate, what prices to charge, and how to examine a customer's genitals for disease. Almost half of Mustang's working girls were considered experienced, having worked as brothel prostitutes for at least three years, and 14 percent of the women were decade-long veterans. Unfortunately, not all of them liked training new prostitutes, claiming their time and effort were wasted on unappreciative amateurs. "Nine times out of ten, you're not going to find anyone who'll use or care about your advice," said Tanya, a thirteen-year Mustang vet. "I don't mind helping a girl with a good head on her shoulders, who doesn't have a problem going in and making sure the man's happy. But I resent being asked to leave the floor to go back to a new girl's room to supervise her and potentially miss a lineup if the girl's only going to ignore me."

Tanya was a forty-one-year-old brunette with a fashionable shag haircut whose petite but sturdy frame commanded attention. And so did her abrupt remarks. She'd been the one on my first visit to brusquely tell me she didn't break condoms. Tanya was tough and at times could sound like a sailor with her crude expletives. A house elder, with a wealth of experience and knowledge about Mustang Ranch, she kept close company with another Mustang veteran, Linda, the prostitute who had expressed considerable disdain for any colleague who enjoyed sex with customers. They hung together in a small clique with two other women of about the same age and seniority. Whether crocheting afghans in the parlor during shift or dining together in the kitchen promptly at six-thirty every night, these women stuck together. They shared a strong sense of common history, and could spend hours chain-smoking and reminiscing about the old days working for Joe and Sally Conforte.

Their eyes sparkled with nostalgia as they described the dress code Sally enforced through the 1980s, which required women to wear long evening gowns covered with rhinestones and sequins and matching gold or silver heels. "And Sally hated black," recalled Linda. "It reminded her of a funeral. Only one girl per shift could wear black." Tanya and Linda laughed as they retold the story of the time Sally came home unexpectedly early from vacation and found a lineup full of black dresses. After chastising the floor maid and women in the middle of the parlor for a good ten minutes, she ordered all the women to strip down and do their lineups for the rest of the night in the nude. Always terrified of Sally, the women complied. "Let this be a lesson to you hos," Sally snapped. "You don't come out here in black."

Old-timers who had worked at Mustang under Sally Conforte reminisced wistfully, not resentfully, about the days when she ruled the roost. Many women believed that Sally's aesthetic standards enhanced their business. "The place had an aura of glamour," said Linda. "The long evening gowns were feminine, and the shiny, glittery rhinestones Hollywood-like. Men felt compelled to spend more money."

The dress code had relaxed considerably since Sally Conforte's day, partly because of the changing of the guard and partly because of changing times. Whereas men and women once dressed up to visit Reno and Vegas's casinos and showrooms, now shorts and T-shirts were ubiquitous. Mustang had relaxed its rules to keep step, and now defined proper dress as "nothing tacky." Specifically, women were to wear underwear at all times, and exposure of nipples or pubic hair was grounds for firing.

Tanya and her friends weren't only nostalgic about brothel attire. They reminisced about the handful of times they had to evacuate the brothel when the nearby Truckee River flooded, and about getting drunk at the Confortes' annual holiday parties, where Joe and Sally gave all the women matching luggage or expensive perfume. But the story they liked to tell best was of being awakened one warm afternoon in 1990 before their shifts started and being told by Joe that the IRS was coming to seize Mustang Ranch for $13 million in unpaid back taxes.

Prostitutes and staff scurried around the brothel, gathering their belongings, like chickens with their heads cut off. When Joe told the women to take anything they could get their hands on, Tanya and Linda frantically began gathering up appliances and pieces of furniture and even filled garbage bags full of frozen meat and vegetables out of the walk-in freezers. In spite of their efforts, most of the brothel's furnishings were confiscated by the IRS and sold in a bankruptcy sale. When Mustang reopened several months later in 1991, the women returned with whatever they rescued from the IRS and proceeded to rebuild the brothel one trick at a time. "The first $50 trick went toward a microwave, and later that night we had enough money to buy towels and groceries," said Linda. "It was a daily thing: 'Come on, girls, we need a toaster!' "

Mustang's newest prostitutes studied Tanya and Linda's clique from a distance, too intimidated to approach any of the women directly. These younger prostitutes said they experienced Tanya and Linda as hostile and dismissive. Unapologetic, Tanya and Linda admitted to standing in judgment of the new breed of prostitutes coming to work at Mustang Ranch. "Us working girls from the old school understand the value of repeat business," said Linda. "We strive to please the guy and make him like us enough to come back to see us again or to tell a buddy about us. We get to know him, ask about his job, his family, and his granddaughter's school project. But with gals starting today, they're just looking at that man as a one-time-only customer and could care less if he comes back. They act like robots in the room, just going through the motions, hurrying to get him out."

The change in women's attitudes over the years had had a negative impact on the business, they contended. "Guys who used to be decent customers and spent decent amounts of money are now becoming cheaper," said Tanya, "because they realize they're not getting a three-hundred-dollar party with a lot of the girls. They're getting the same as if they spent a hundred bucks. It doesn't matter if they spent a hundred bucks or a thousand; those girls have got them out the door in twenty minutes." The telltale sign of a woman's professionalism, Tanya said, was how the man acted when he emerged from her bedroom. "If he comes out walking real fast, twenty feet in front of her, nine times out of ten, he really didn't enjoy himself, and will probably never come back again."

Linda took a slow drag on her cigarette before adding, "But these new girls don't care; they figure they're young and there's always gonna be somebody walking through that door. They think their pussies are lined with platinum! If they only bothered to listen to what us girls who've been in the business a long time have told them—that eventually they're gonna be our age sitting where I am, with one customer while the new girl gets ten. They're going to be thankful for that one customer. We aren't trying to be mean or vindictive. We're just trying to make sure there's guys coming back. If there ain't business coming in, there's no need for any of us to be here." With that, she stubbed out her Salem Light into a plastic red ashtray and lit up another.

When I asked gingerly whether either woman felt envious of the younger girls, Linda defensively rejected the idea. "I don't trip out on how often a younger girl gets picked versus me. I can't compare myself to youth, to an eighteen- or nineteen-year-old. There's no way. I'm satisfied with what I'm making and whatever she's banking is her business." She quickly added, "What she makes is what I used to make!"

Tanya was more forthright about her demons. "I think I'm going through a phase right now, a little insecurity about my age and the younger girls in here. I think anybody over thirty goes through it, especially as vain as women are. But then I turn around and sometimes make off one date what takes the younger girls ten dates. So, it all evens out."

It wasn't just the new, younger prostitutes who felt excluded and ignored by Tanya and Linda. Older, seasoned Mustang workers, like Baby, who shared the women's same history also found themselves left out of their clique. Baby's crowd consisted principally of night-shift workers, who tended to have wilder, more outgoing personalities. There was Daisy, an in-your-face prankster who liked to entertain her peers with parodies. One night she passed around homemade ballots so that everyone could vote on recipients of various farcical awards. Categories included "Whore You Don't Even Know Has a Job Here (Because She's Never on the Floor)," and "Whore That Is Banned from the Jukebox for Life (Because She Only Plays Crap)." Then there was Baby's friend Selena, who couldn't keep anyone's name straight, only their astrological sign. She greeted me each evening with "Hello, Aquarius."

Drugs also connected many of these night girls. Although brothel rules prohibited illegal substances, use of marijuana, crank, cocaine, and crack did occur. Management tried to control the influx of drugs by having floor maids randomly search women's belongings when they first arrived and then when they returned from vacation. They also required prostitutes to turn over all prescription medications, which were locked in the cashier's office to prevent theft. While the house threatened dismissal of any woman caught in possession of drugs, I came to see that managers rarely enforced that rule. As for alcohol, the official Mustang rules stated: "In this house, it is a privilege to drink, act accordingly. If the bartender or the floor maid feels that you have had enough to drink, don't argue!"

Nevertheless, drinking and drugging often helped some of Mustang's women cope with anxiety, boredom, and long work hours. Initially, women tried to hide their use of drugs from me, but as they grew more comfortable, they began letting down their guard and started getting stoned and cutting up their crank in front of me. One night, I had a talk with Mercedes, the woman who had a strange relationship with her regular named Gary. We sat at the bar, where I usually watched her overspend on drinks each night, and she ranted about the evils of alcohol, or "the devil in disguise" as she called it, and how Mustang shouldn't allow women like herself—those with little self-control—to drink at all. "It's the fear of being rejected that makes you drink in here. And the fear of sitting here quietly trying to look at the four walls that drives you to drink in here. You know if you bring out your book they [management] are gonna tell you to close it, so you come over here to the bar and drink instead."

Regardless of its prevalence among a subset of the working girls, drug use was far more controlled than what I had seen among the juvenile prostitutes of Times Square. Still, while some of these women had come to the brothels already addicted, quite a few, sadly, embarked on their drug and alcohol habits while at Mustang.

Many of the working girls didn't fit into any particular social group. One such woman was Dinah, Mustang's oldest prostitute (sixty-three), who preferred to keep to herself. Reticent about her outside life, Dinah found Tanya and Linda's group too chatty and Baby's clique too unruly. Described by her colleagues as "Mustang's straightest prostitute," Dinah abstained from not only alcohol and drugs, but also caffeine, and limited her intake of processed sugar. Dinah even paid her taxes. "When I first got hired, I went to my accountant and told him I was a hooker," Dinah explained to me once. "I said I didn't know how to go about doing my taxes. I heard everyone else say not to bother." Inexperienced in such matters, her accountant called the IRS, who counseled him to declare her a "registered professional entertainer." Last year, Dinah got back $1,100. "Imagine me, a hooker, getting money back from the government," she said, chuckling.

In many ways, management reinforced the brothel's cliquishness and competitive tension. I remembered distinctly Irene's admonishment to new prostitutes: "This is a cutthroat place. You're here to make money, not friends." While Irene's words of caution were well intentioned, they served to perpetuate the underlying distrust between the women. When I asked the women why they hadn't organized to form a union or joined together to purchase a brothel themselves, most of the prostitutes rolled their eyes and said they could never trust "another ho."

Brothel staff also seemed to benefit from the women's rivalries and discords. Women offered management and workers gifts and financial kickbacks in order to gain preferential treatment. Most offered money voluntarily, in the hope of earning special privileges and keeping brothel authorities out of their hair. As one woman put it, "I pay my 'insurance' at the beginning of the week because I don't know what sort of shit is going to happen to me; I might need the indemnity." But staff members were also notorious for pressuring prostitutes into making payoffs. Speculating that the Nair incident could have only occurred with the tacit approval of a floor maid, one of the bartenders encouraged Heather to start tipping all of Mustang's floor maids extra to buy their loyalty.

Despite how antagonistic relations between brothel prostitutes could be, there was another side to the story. Along with jealousy and competition, I also found camaraderie and real solidarity. Although the women didn't articulate their support for one another very often, they demonstrated it in a number of other ways.

One day I saw Tanya, who had been so outspoken about her hatred of training newcomers, pull aside a young turn-out to warn her that one of Mustang's more infamous regulars had just come in. Tim the Barker was a wealthy local bachelor who was renowned throughout the Storey County brothels for his special tic: he barked like a dog when he had an orgasm. New prostitutes who hadn't been informed in advance were known to panic, mistaking Tim's yaps for a seizure. Those alerted ahead of time usually managed to remain calm. "Even though Tanya warned me about him," the turn-out later told me, "when he started barking like a schnauzer, I almost died—I thought he was going to bite me."

Crisis also drew the women together. One day everyone in the parlor heard a panic buzzer go off, an eerie, shrill sound that resounded through the brothel like an air-raid siren. Within moments, a woman could be heard screaming in one of the rooms. Because the women at Mustang took pride in controlling their own parties and didn't resort to using the buzzers hidden at the base of their beds very often, everyone in the house knew to take this signal seriously. (Allegedly, no woman has ever been seriously hurt at Mustang Ranch.*) Immediately, the bartender and cook—both men—rushed from their stations down Hallway C in the direction of the screams. As was typically the case, a customer had become belligerent when he was too drunk to maintain an erection. To save face, he had decided to blame the prostitute, pinning her down on the bed with one arm and striking her with his one free fist. Luckily, the bartender and cook pulled him off the woman

---

*There has only been one reported case of assault against a prostitute in a Nevada brothel in the last twenty-one years. In contrast, one 1998 study of San Francisco prostitutes found that 82 percent had been physically assaulted since entering prostitution (55 percent by their customers), and 68 percent had been raped (46 percent by their customers).

before he seriously hurt her. Although brothel management sometimes called in the local sheriff in cases such as this one, they simply threw out this customer—literally—into the parking lot outside Mustang's gates, and ordered him never to return. Back inside, women clustered around the woman who had been assaulted to comfort her. A few prostitutes even interrupted their parties, leaving customers alone back in their rooms, to console their colleague. All the women could identify with the distress of being victimized by a customer, and no one held back any empathy.

The women also came together in times of celebration. Tiffany's baby shower was a case in point. When she got pregnant by her boyfriend, this Mustang prostitute of eight years decided to keep working to save cash until she began showing at about six months. When she finally "came off the floor," management offered Tiffany a job as day cashier so she wouldn't fall too behind in her bills. Before she quit this job, just before her delivery, the other prostitutes threw her a surprise baby shower.

The women decorated the ceiling and walls of Mustang #1's kitchen with white balloons and blue, pink, yellow, and green streamers. Sarah, the day bartender, baked a flat chocolate cake and decorated it with vanilla frosting and a candied carousel. The women and staff had all chipped in to buy Tiffany a slew of gifts, from a bassinet and stroller to a playpen and hamper, each brimming over with still more presents, all gift-wrapped in paper decorated with pastel storks and teddy bears. They must have spent close to $1,000. When Tiffany was led into the room, it was apparent from her stunned expression, trembling lips, and tearing eyes, that she was deeply moved by her colleagues' generosity.

We nibbled on cake and watched as Tiffany opened her gifts while new customers were forced to wait in the bar. We oohed and ahhed as she unwrapped baby booties, bibs, blankets, and even a couple of handmade afghans crocheted by house elders like Linda and Tanya. When Tiffany came upon a pair of infant swim shorts in leopard-print Lycra, one of the women kidded, "For your hooker child." The room broke into gales of laughter.

The event that gave off the greatest feeling of kinship among the women was Tanya and Linda's joint birthday party, the year they turned forty-two and forty-one, respectively. The party had become a brothel tradition in the more than ten years that both women had worked at Mustang. Recently they had begun calling it the old-timers' party. There were days of planning and prep work, with women sneaking in bottles of liquor past those floor maids and members of management who didn't approve.

The party began on a Saturday night around eight o'clock, back in a free bedroom. Only Tanya and Linda's small clique and a few other women were initially included, but the festivities opened up about an hour later, when the partiers came running into the parlor in the midst of a heated Silly String and water balloon fight. The rest of us looked on in astonishment to see the house elders acting so carefree and youthful, uncharacteristically indifferent to the customers and business at hand.

The rest of us were then invited down for "purple hooters," concocted of vodka, sweet-and-sour (or lime), and

156 ·· ALEXA ALBERT

Chambord raspberry liqueur. Tanya made a toast to all the women over forty years old still working in the business. Then, in an effort to inspire, she added that the younger girls could also work to that age if they so desired. Others followed with more toasts, many acknowledging each other as "real hos"—prostitutes who knew trade secrets for satisfying any man—and for being good businesswomen who maintained their senses of humor and had the guts to wear big wigs.

As the women got tipsier, they grew more sentimental and began reminiscing. "Remember the time when there was that explosion across the highway and they evacuated the whole valley? Joe and David [Burgess, owner of the Old Bridge Ranch] put us all up in the Hilton." Others jumped in. "News of our coming spread like wildfire. People playing the slot machines and blackjack just gawked when over fifty of us girls walked through that casino. Like, Oh my God, look at all the Mustang prostitutes!" And, "Boy did we have a party that night. Our attitude was, We got a day off!"

At one point, someone noticed that Dinah hadn't come down to join the festivities. I wasn't surprised, because she didn't feel very comfortable with Tanya's clique and also didn't drink alcohol. "Somebody go get Dinah," Tanya yelled, chugging down another purple hooter. Dinah was as much a part of Mustang's sisterhood as anyone else, Tanya went on to explain, and she needed to join the rest of them in celebration. When Dinah finally entered the room and the other working girls broke into applause, an embarrassed but pleased expression crept over her face. To be a good sport, she even offered up a toast and drank a purple hooter.

Suddenly, Mercedes, who had been busy with a customer and missed much of the party, barged into the room, dragging behind her a scrawny-looking man half her height wearing lopsided glasses and wrapped in a sheet, toga-style. "It's his birthday today too," Mercedes proclaimed. She began singing "Happy Birthday" in her high-pitched Michael Jackson voice, then all of a sudden she yanked off the man's toga to reveal his naked body, erect penis, and sweat-beaded chest. The room roared with laughter. Amid the hoots and catcalls, someone yelled out an offer of $50 for a fuck. The poor man blushed at all the attention and the women cheered him on for his good sportsmanship. The party went on (without Mercedes's customer) into the early hours of the next day. Although not much business got done, the women viewed the evening as a total success.

Theirs was a strange circumstance—to be competing fiercely with one another while also sharing a deep sense of solidarity. Brittany put it succinctly: "I love these women here, even my enemies. Even if we don't like each other, we're still on the same team. We'll protect each other, because we're all working girls."

In truth, few outsiders—family members or otherwise—could truly identify with the prostitutes or offer them support. Despite their legal status in Nevada, many women returned to homes in different states where prostitution was still criminalized. Given the social stigma of prostitution, these women kept their work secret from neighbors and square friends, making it difficult to establish honest relationships in their home communities. Most of the prostitutes I spoke with told me they had decided long ago not to establish outside friendships, so they wouldn't have to lie about what they did for a living. In fact, I was learning that even in Nevada, where brothels were historic, legal institutions, licensed prostitutes still faced considerable condemnation.

7 .. LEGALIZED, NOT LEGITIMIZED

One summer night, George Flint and his wife, Bette, invited me to their home to celebrate their granddaughter Lisa's fifteenth birthday. I had come to feel close to the Flints, who seemed to appreciate my sincere, nonjudgmental curiosity. George was thrilled to have someone as interested in the brothels as he, and Bette was glad that her husband had someone willing to listen. I had been flattered to be included in this family event, at which I would finally get to meet Bette's daughter, Marlene. I had already become acquainted with Lisa, Marlene's daughter, and I was eager to meet as many of the family as I could.

The night started off badly. Marlene was clearly in a foul mood, and George told me later that she was furious at him for bringing Lisa along when he picked me up at Mustang Ranch. Lisa had seen Mustang Ranch only once before, as a small child, when George had pointed it out from the highway. Marlene had always tried to shield her child from the brothels and downplayed the fact that Lisa's grandfather ran the state's brothel association. Now that Lisa was a teenager, and inevitably beginning to pull away from home, I imagined Marlene's anxiety mounting. If anything, Marlene's overzealousness could have the opposite effect, I feared; many a rebellious teenager finds a parent's worst fears tempting if not irresistible.

Conversation during dinner was light, dominated by George's gossip about the "business" at Mustang Ranch. Throughout the evening, I sensed Marlene's eyes creeping over my face. There was something accusatory about her gaze that made me increasingly uneasy. I knew that Marlene had never in her life consented to visit a brothel with her stepfather, and I imagined that she thought I had been tainted by my involvement. By her standards, maybe I had.

I was interested to know more about her attitude, so after dinner I asked her and her brother, Dean, to share some of their thoughts about the brothels, as family members of an industry bigwig and as local citizens. Dean and Marlene had very different opinions, and as we got into it, Marlene grew visibly more uncomfortable. She rolled her eyes almost continuously as Dean, now forty years old, described the thrill and excitement he had felt as a young man growing up in the only state in the Union with the "guts" to legalize prostitution.

Marlene interrupted and asked, with a touch of hostility, why I was so interested in the topic. I explained that in the process of conducting a public health study, I had discovered that essentially no research, either sociological or health related, had been done in Nevada brothels, and the time seemed ripe. Again, Marlene rolled her eyes and said nothing, but her body language shouted "Liar." I tried to explain that my earlier studies had focused on condom use. "That's enough, stop!" Marlene yelped. "My daughter's in this house."

Without missing a beat, Dean volunteered that as a teenager he had patronized the brothels. "You didn't have to worry about going to a party in junior high or high school and having that pressure of trying to have sex with someone," he said.

That was over the top for Marlene. "I think there's a time and a place for some things," she shrieked, jumping up. "My daughter's here, and Dean, I know you would never be talking about these things in front of *your* children."

Actually, Lisa was nowhere to be seen. She was watching television with her grandfather in another room behind a closed door, completely out of earshot. It was Marlene herself who brought the conversation to Lisa when she got up and stomped into the television room to announce her raw feelings about me to George.

She declared that she was offended by my insensitivity to the situation—my lack of discretion in discussing this topic under the same roof as Lisa—and that my interest in these women and my support and tolerance for them were inconceivable.

Not to mention that I was actually socializing and cohabiting with them!

The night ended dismally, with George angry at Marlene, Marlene angry at Dean, Dean angry at Marlene, and me angry at human nature. George reassured me that Marlene's attack on me was merely a camouflaged attack on him and the brothel industry that paid him to represent and defend it. All I could think about was George telling me on the first day we met that he'd once offered to arrange a visit to one of the brothels for Marlene's high school boyfriend "if the boy needed some."

Still, I felt sorry for George. He had been dealing with his family's strict judgment his entire life. His parents, both of whom were ordained ministers in a fundamentalist and Pentecostal Christian church, had ruled their household with iron fists. George's sneak visit to his high school prom was quashed when his father showed up and pulled his humiliated son off the dance floor, leaving his date standing there alone. George's parents were now in their late eighties, and they knew nothing about his brothel job.

I was relieved to get back to Mustang Ranch that night. It felt safe and warm, and the place where I belonged, where I didn't feel judged. I was wrung out by my encounter with Marlene. I suspected that Marlene felt overwhelmed and extremely frustrated by the lack of sympathy and understanding in the room that night. But she had shaken me up, demoralized me. I could only imagine how she would have made me feel if I were a Mustang prostitute.

Until that night, I had almost managed to forget how controversial prostitution was in mainstream America. Legalized prostitution had started making sense to me, particularly in terms of the safety it provided women. Because there were legalized brothels in most of Nevada, I assumed the majority of Nevadans had come to tolerate and even accept them. Without having to do much digging at all, though, I quickly came to see that Marlene was but one voice in a chorus of local opposition. Legality was no assurance of legitimacy.

After my evening with Marlene, I decided to look into the Nevada opposition. Immediately, I discovered John Reese. He was the brothel industry's most notorious foe, and his name appeared regularly in the *Reno Gazette-Journal*. A fifty-four-year-old Reno construction worker, he had been furiously crusading for over a decade to rid Nevada of its legalized brothels. He refused to meet me, but he did agree to a telephone interview.

He began the conversation by offering that he hadn't always been a crusader. In fact, when he was younger, he used to patronize Joe Conforte's pre-Mustang brothels. After becoming a born-again Christian in his mid-thirties, however, he became obsessed with repenting for his former sins and getting brothel prostitution outlawed. Over his ten years of activism, Reese estimated, he had spent over $35,000 of his own money to fund his various campaigns, from petition drives (all of which ultimately fell short) to lobbying legislators under the auspices of his organization, Nevadans Against Prostitution (membership unknown). (George Flint calculates that Reese has spent over $150,000.) Reese attributed his unblemished string of failures to the fact that politicians and the public "see us as a pest and a nuisance, a bunch of religious people trying to shut down the brothels." In fact, say Reese's critics, he is his own worst enemy. They say it has been his "false claims of Christian love" and capricious methods of attack that have deterred potential allies, like religious and women's groups, from aligning with him.

There's some truth to this. Reese has changed tactics the way some people change hairstyles. Once he attacked legalized prostitution solely on religious and moral grounds. Then he tried to frighten the public with allegations about concealed health hazards in the brothels. He leased two billboards on opposite sides of Interstate 80 near the exit to Mustang Ranch and put up ads reading, WARNING: BROTHELS ARE NOT AIDS SAFE. When George and the Nevada Brothel Association threatened to sue Reese and the 3M National Advertising Company, which leased the billboards for $1,500 a month, for libel, the advertising company painted over the billboards. Reese should have known full well that his allegations were false. Since March 1986, when the state's Bureau of Disease Control and Intervention Services began requiring brothel prostitutes to undergo monthly HIV tests, over 53,000 such tests have been conducted, and no licensed prostitute has ever tested positive.* (Twenty-six brothel applicants have tested HIV-positive, have been denied work cards, and are barred for life from employment as legal prostitutes.)

---

*As early as 1985, nearly three-fourths of Nevada's brothels voluntarily started testing their prostitutes for HIV after business dropped 30 to 50 percent as a consequence of heightened publicity about the disease. Not until 1988, after the institution of the mandatory condom law, did business fully rebound.

When Reese's fear tactics failed, he tried a different approach. In 1994, he stepped down as president of Nevadans Against Prostitution, and announced he was seeking a license to open Nevada's first gay brothel. Reese seemed to have undergone a radical conversion, publicly claiming that "the brothels are a good place for gays to go to have safe sex." Declaring that Nevada could become "the gay prostitution capital of the nation," Reese pledged that the state would soon have two gay brothels and "as many as ten or more within the next five years."

Playing to local homophobia was shrewd. Even George admitted that with this tactic Reese had finally succeeded in getting under the skin of the brothel industry. State statutes criminalizing gay and lesbian sex had been repealed in 1993, and there were no county codes to prohibit gay brothels. As George pointed out, the brothel industry couldn't outright oppose a gay brothel without appearing to be discriminatory, but Reese's proposal could very well prompt the legislature to ban brothels entirely. Only after the Nye County commissioners turned down Reese's application because it was incomplete did Reese withdraw his proposal, admitting he was only trying to bring attention to his antiprostitution agenda.

In 1999, Reese pulled off his most outlandish stunt yet. He staged his own abduction, leaving his car running near Mustang Ranch with a door window broken out and bloodstains, presumably his, inside, suggesting foul play. Police spent the next ten days on a wild-goose chase, searching for Reese with deputies, dogs, and a helicopter. Three days after his disappearance, a security camera at a Sacramento bank recorded him withdrawing money from his account. After the fact, of course, he admitted that his vanishing had been staged to draw attention to his battle. This time, the public was far less amused; the Washoe county sheriff's office billed him the $8,761 spent to finance the search.

Remarkably, he hadn't alienated everyone, and he had the support of even a few Nevada politicians, including State Senator William O'Donnell, a Republican from Las Vegas. In fact, during our phone call, Reese credited O'Donnell with being "sort of a father to the antibrothel movement." Privately, O'Donnell allegedly had encouraged Reese to stick to AIDS fear tactics because "morals didn't seem to work in Nevada." (Reese's organization ultimately returned the favor and gave O'Donnell a $2,000 campaign contribution.)

Eager to meet a politician who publicly opposed the brothels, I called O'Donnell's office in Las Vegas and to my surprise got him on the phone. I explained that I was a medical student who had done some public health research at Mustang Ranch and now was exploring the larger social ramifications of legalized prostitution, and that a number of politicians had recommended I contact him. Wanting to conceal my bias for as long as possible, I didn't mention that I had been *living* at Mustang Ranch off and on. To my surprise, instead of giving me the brush-off, he said he would be pleased to talk to me.

The day of our meeting, I arrived early at the Las Vegas real estate agency that O'Donnell ran in his spare time. Nevada legislators had lots of spare time, because the state legislature was in session only six months every year (in 1999 this was reduced to four months). Spare time hadn't made O'Donnell prompt, however. He kept me waiting in the reception area for over half an hour while he finished some business. When his secretary finally escorted me back to his office, O'Donnell didn't look up to greet me but continued poring over his papers. After a few minutes, he began tidying up the documents and stood to shake my hand. "That article was about some sleazeball who has been ripping off young, poor women with realty scams," he said, explaining his tardiness.

Sitting as a state senator for twelve years—he represented Las Vegas District 5-South and West Vegas—had obviously made the forty-seven-year-old media-savvy. He wouldn't let me record our interview, reasoning, "I don't know what you are going to use that tape for." I put the recorder away. Ten minutes into the interview he stopped himself mid-sentence and asked, "Sure you're not taping this?" His suspiciousness reminded me of John Reese's reluctance to meet me in person. How strange, I thought, that brothel opponents were more apprehensive about speaking to a stranger than members of the brothel industry had been.

Our interview was initially unremarkable. O'Donnell recalled that he first laid eyes on a brothel in 1973, when he drove past the four brothels outside Carson City, the state capital. In 1985 as a freshman assemblyman, he got his first taste of the legislature's tacit support of the brothels when assemblywoman Barbara Zimmer, a Republican from Las Vegas, introduced a bill to outlaw prostitution, and he watched as her bill "went nowhere." Troubled by this, O'Donnell said he tried as a state senator in 1987 to pass another bill banning brothels statewide. But O'Donnell quickly realized that, like Zimmer, he couldn't get enough votes. "The standard reaction I got was that the brothels were a local option. The rural politicians and liberals asked, 'What are you doing legislating in my district?' Since I couldn't get any support, I dropped the whole thing. I'm disgusted with the whole situation."

O'Donnell has threatened in three different legislative sessions to introduce legislation to close the brothels, he told me frankly, but he has concluded that all attempts to legislate will be futile until "we change people's attitudes," meaning their morality. Calling Nevada "an unchurch state," O'Donnell informed me that more than 70 percent of the state's population lacked affiliation to a church or organized religion. O'Donnell also said he was offended by the culture's sexism. "It bothers me that we're making money off the backs of women. Condoning prostitution is the most demeaning and degrading thing the state can do to women. What we do as a state is essentially put a U.S.-grade stamp on the butt of every prostitute. Instead, we should be turning them around by helping them get back into society."

I perked up at this. What did he have in mind? What did he propose doing to help these women? "Nothing," he said. "There are already so many community programs out there. Anyone with half a brain could get services." When I pointed out that such services were usually only short-term, he replied, "If you give them long-term help, they'll be imprisoned for life."

O'Donnell believed that legalized prostitution encourged men and women to transgress the social mores that kept us civilized, that kept us Christian. "I've been married twenty-three years," he said. "We've had knock-down, drag-out fights. If you have other releases or escapes, like brothels, you don't need to be pulled back to the marriage, and divorce is just a matter of time. Brothels make marriages weaker. The government shouldn't make it easier for men to step out on their wives and encourage divorce."

But brothels only existed, I said, in response to the preexisting demand; some men intended to buy sex, whether it was legal or not. O'Donnell's eyes lit up. "Oh, economics. I got my bachelor's in economics," he said patronizingly. "Supply and demand. What is the point of equilibrium? When supply equals demand. Prostitution upsets this equilibrium. I don't have to get into a relationship with a woman because any day of the week I can get some sex from a prostitute."

We had been talking for nearly two hours. We were both on the edge of our seats; the room pulsed with energy, pent up as well as released, and with a palpable intellectual tension. A bead of perspiration formed on his receding hairline and saliva had gathered in the corners of his mouth. Suddenly, O'Donnell steered the conversation off prostitution. "I bet you're pro-abortion," he said. "Well, I'm pro-life and proud of it. As a senator, I'm more interested in representing the defenseless, the unprepared, and the vulnerable of this world. People like me are trying to pull the world to what's righteous and produces life, not death or mental destruction.

"You're a medical student. You understand physics. Here's the light spectrum." He was panting now. "You have blue, ultraviolet, red, etc. Blue is heaven, and red is hell. Human beings are somewhere on the line between. As they move towards the blue, they are more divine, more devout, like St. Francis, whose whole life was dedicated to being more divine than animal. People who enjoy being more animal than divine are more towards red, or hell. Should government encourage man to be more animal or more divine?"

I was now late for another interview. O'Donnell stood to follow me out, determined to have the last word in his final campaign to offer me salvation. "Your intellect will keep you from knowing the truth," he yelled from the curbside as I got in my rental car. As I pulled out, through the glass I saw O'Donnell mouth the words, "The truth is, it's Wrong."

Other brothel critics packaged their condemnation in more pragmatic terms. There was the magnate Steve Wynn, owner of the Golden Nugget, Treasure Island, Mirage, and Bellagio casinos and arguably the most influential businessman in Nevada, who asserted that legalized prostitution tarnished the state's image and deterred new enterprise.* "We have outgrown legalized prostitution," wrote Wynn in a letter he sent to all Nevada state senators and assembly members in 1988. "The existence of brothels in Nevada is just one more item

---

*In 2000, Wynn sold his gaming holdings for $1 billion and acquired the old and famous Desert Inn as a birthday present for his wife. He subsequently closed the property with plans to raze the building and erect his most lavish casino-resort yet.

that out-of-state media people use to denigrate the quality of life in Nevada. . . . It is not good for Nevada's image to have wide-open legalized 'cat houses' and the sooner we put that image behind us, the better we will be." At risk, he threatened, were tourism and gaming revenues; the latter produced monthly taxable revenues of $632 million in 1997.

How ironic that a casino czar should accuse the brothels of soiling Nevada's image. Since the days of Bugsy Siegel (the notorious mobster who built Las Vegas's first casino, the Flamingo Hotel), sex had been promoted as an essential accompaniment to gambling, from the lavish showgirl revues and provocatively dressed cocktail waitresses to the bell captains and pit bosses brokering sex between customers and house girls. Despite Wynn's contention that his industry had been cleaned up and the casinos transformed into ideal family vacation spots, Las Vegas's freelance sex market flourished, with *140 pages* of the Las Vegas Yellow Pages devoted to "Entertainers"—much to the chagrin of the brothel industry, which was prohibited from advertising. But whereas the brothels drew men out of the casinos, the freelancers worked inside and kept gamblers on the premises. I suspected that what Wynn really disliked was the idea of losing customers to the legal brothels.

Economic arguments like Wynn's met resistance primarily from rural legislators, who had their own fiscal reasons for endorsing legalized prostitution. In 1998, Nevada's local governments received over $500,000 from brothel business licenses, liquor licenses, and work cards. This was over and above revenue from property taxes, initial investigation fees upon application for brothel licenses, and room and boarding licenses in certain counties. Storey County received $182,500 in revenue from its brothels, Mustang Ranch and Old Bridge Ranch, a sum amounting to almost 4 percent of the county's total general fund.

Brothels also provided jobs. Mustang Ranch was Storey County's third largest employer, after the Kal Kan dog food factory and the school district, and had an annual payroll of $1.3 million, employing seventy-five people in positions ranging from floor maids to maintenance helpers. Local suppliers who provided goods and services directly to the brothels all benefited financially, as did taxicab drivers. And the need for police expenditure on vice squads was largely eliminated, because illegal prostitution was virtually nonexistent in counties that permitted brothels.

More disputable, however, were claims by brothel members that legalized prostitution reduced the incidence of local sex crimes by offering potential perpetrators safe environments to act out aberrant sexual fantasies that might otherwise endanger the public. Women had told me about the men with pedophile fantasies who paid them to dress up and pretend to be little girls. My running partner Heather had a regular who asked her to pretend to be his daughter and say things like, "Fuck me, Daddy. I won't tell Mommy." She hoped that because he came to see her, he wouldn't go out and molest a real child.

But others were more skeptical that the brothels could reduce child abuse and rape. According to *Nevada Crime Statis-*

tics, the state experienced significantly higher rates of sex crimes than the rest of the nation throughout the 1990s.*

Brothel opponents like Wynn, O'Donnell, and Reese have accused the "influential and monied" Nevada Brothel Association (NBA) of propagating "self-serving" misinformation about the industry, making untrue claims that sex crimes had diminished and exaggerating the brothels' economic impact. George Flint said he took offense at such allegations. The NBA never lobbied for legalized prostitution per se, he asserted. Instead, it took the libertarian position that brothels were age-old state institutions whose regulation was traditionally left to local governmental bodies. "All the bills that have been introduced tried to make prostitution illegal across the board," George explained to me one afternoon in Mustang #1's bar. "Nuts and bolts, bottom line, we say, That's an impractical way for you to legislate, because even though there may be reasons to outlaw brothel prostitution in Washoe County, there may be reasons to keep it legal in another county."

The history of George's involvement with the brothel industry is instructive, because it also charts the ebb and flow

---

*For example, in 1997, Nevada's rate of forcible rape per 1,000 population was .57, while the national rate was .36. Despite the proximity of Mustang Ranch and Old Bridge Ranch to Reno and Sparks, the two cities documented a total of 144 rapes in 1997, or .64 per 1,000 population, almost two times the national rate. While some Nevada state officials contend that the state's tourists—42 million in 1997—inflated these statistics, Nevada's two biggest metropolitan areas, Reno and Las Vegas, ranked far ahead of other popular American tourist cities, including Los Angeles and San Francisco, in rapes. (Still, in Nevada's defense, the atmosphere of tourism *is* characteristically different in this state from most others.)

of its opponents' fortunes. A handful of brothel owners approached George in 1985 looking for a leader. Since relocating to Nevada from Oregon twenty years earlier and opening his wedding chapel, George had become a respected and effective lobbyist, first for the wedding chapel industry and later for other interest groups, including physicians and employment agencies. George had been well aware that the brothel industry had no "presence" in the legislature, except for Joe Conforte, who regularly made political campaign contributions to candidates statewide. When Rock Hudson's death raised public awareness of AIDS, George predicted that the brothels would have to work in concert to protect their interests or risk losing the industry altogether.

Not all of George's friends and colleagues in the legislature agreed that a brothel association would be a good thing. An association and lobbyist meant heightened visibility for a state institution that may have been tolerated but still carried with it considerable baggage. Sure, almost all professional and business groups had associations, politicians told George, from bankers and gamers to embalmers and funeral directors, but the brothels were different—they were *whorehouses*. But legislators were soothed by the notion of having George at the helm, a lobbyist they considered reasonable. "Lawmakers knew I wasn't a flash in a pan," said George. "They knew I wouldn't go half-crazy and start marching hookers through the halls of the legislature."

Aware of how controversial his new clients were, George approached lawmakers with caution. Thus his decision never to suggest to legislators that prostitution was good or that whorehouses should be more widely distributed. Instead, he took the position that lawmakers should continue respecting the state's age-old belief in decentralized government, its emphasis on local control and personal liberties. This gave lawmakers a way to support his clients without appearing to be in favor of legalized prostitution. "Rather than come out openly as soft on prostitution or pro-brothel, legislators could say that local authorities are in a better position to make that decision," George explained to me. "My goal as lobbyist is never to see a bill make it to the point where individual members, our friends, are embarrassed by having to take a public stand on the rise or fall of legalized prostitution."

George was just as careful in doling out political contributions. Although most politicians were more than willing to accept money from the brothels, they preferred not to do so publicly. Because Nevada permits candidates to receive contributions of up to $500 without naming the donor publicly, George made all his political action contributions in checks of $500 or less. If the NBA wanted to give a senator a $2,000 contribution, George sent four checks, each for $500 from four different brothels. In the NBA's first year, half a dozen checks were returned to George. In recent years, the number has dwindled to one or two.

When I told him that O'Donnell and Reese accused the NBA of "bribing" politicians, George raised his voice a decibel and told me that the brothels were no different from any other interest group that made political contributions, except that the NBA spent far less money than other industries, especially gaming. In 1996, the NBA contributed approximately $50,000 to legislators' campaigns (nearly 60 percent coming from Mustang Ranch), while the gaming industry dispensed $800,000 to statewide legislative races. "It's crude to say," George added, "but at all levels of politics, money's the name of the game. One hand washes the other. It's that simple. The brothel business survives on politics, friendship, and political action contributions."

I appreciated George's shrewdness, but the fact that the executive director of the NBA felt it necessary to beat around the bush with legislators about a lawful profession bothered me. It seemed to me that the merits of legalized prostitution spoke for themselves, and that sidestepping the issue—making it one of political jurisdiction—undermined their validity.

But for the time being, Nevadans seemed to favor the status quo, or so said multiple public opinion polls. In a 1986 telephone survey of registered voters in northern Nevada, 66 percent said they believed the state should leave the right to legalize brothels with each county, letting voters have a direct say on the issue. As of the year 2002, only southeast Nevada's Lincoln County had voted (by public referendum) to repeal its existing law legalizing brothels. General opinion held that the brothels were tolerable, as long as they kept a low profile. What seemed to worry citizens were the brothels that became too well known, which usually happened when owners refused to remain discreet. The most notorious, of course, was Joe Conforte.

Even after getting brothel prostitution legalized in 1971, Conforte didn't stop thumbing his nose at the establishment. A national folk hero of sorts, Conforte wallowed in the ensuing media attention, much to the chagrin of conservative Nevadans. In 1972, *Rolling Stone* magazine ran a cover story entitled "Joe Conforte, Crusading Pimp: A Concerned Citizen's Fight to Keep Prostitutes Off the Streets of Nevada." Long critical of flashy brothel publicity, the *Reno Gazette-Journal* published editorial after editorial condemning Conforte. (The newspaper, then named the *Reno Evening Gazette*, actually won a Pulitzer Prize for Editorial Writing in 1977 for a series of editorials on Joe Conforte, his Mustang Ranch brothel, and his alleged influence on Washoe County public officials.)

One editorial published in 1976 read, "If Conforte wishes to run a whorehouse, he can do it as everyone else does it: quietly. Conforte needs to get the message that Reno does not want him to ride in its parades, finance its bus lines, influence its politicians, or be front row center as the gamblers celebrate him with the best showroom tables." (To curry favor, brothel owners have traditionally made donations ranging from uniforms for local Little League teams to bulletproof vests for county sheriff departments.)

A classic example of Conforte's grandstanding was the time he showed off his patriotism by offering single servicemen stationed in the Persian Gulf free twenty-four-hour dates with Mustang prostitutes upon their return. Such a party normally cost about $1,000. "I'm going to give them the ultimate morale booster," Conforte told the press. In the end, between 100 and 150 servicemen took advantage of Conforte's offer. "He was such an animal for publicity," George told me. "It didn't make a difference whether he made a good impression or not, because Joe worked under the theory that any publicity was good publicity."

But some kinds of publicity could be damaging, even to Conforte. In 1976, the Argentine heavyweight boxer Oscar Bonavena, once the world's fifth-ranked contender (58 and 9, with 43 knockouts), was shot and killed in the parking lot of Mustang Ranch allegedly by Conforte's bodyguard, Willard Ross Brymer. At the time, Mustang's arsenal included two AR-15s, three 12-gauge shotguns, a Mace gun, and sidearms for all security guards. Rumor had it that Conforte had emerged from the brothel after the shooting and shouted, "Move this fucking bloody body from the door to my brothel!"*

Although Conforte was not implicated in the killing, he was assumed to have some connection to it, especially after the media unearthed evidence of an affair between Bonavena and Conforte's wife. (Among other suspicious events, the body had been moved by the time the medical examiner arrived, so no firm conclusions could be drawn as to where the killer had stood.) Conforte took further heat when the ensuing criminal investigation was deemed insufficient because of his interference. Two grand jury investigations concluded that Conforte held "unusual influence and power" over county officials, naming the district attorney, Virgil Bucchianeri, and the sheriff,

---

*Brymer pleaded guilty to voluntary manslaughter and served sixteen months in prison.

Bob Del Carlo, both of whom handled the Bonavena investigation. Conforte's lavish entertaining, free brothel passes, and campaign contributions had corrupted county government, critics contended.

Conforte's influence over county politics was due, in part, to his ability to tip elections. Allegedly, he had engineered a bloc of votes, the "river vote," comprised of Mustang Ranch staff and prostitutes (whose legal residence may or may not have been in-county) and tenants in his Lockwood Mobile Home Park, a community of ninety-four low-rent trailers and single-family houses that he had developed. Storey County had only 2,500 residents, and fewer than 1,500 registered voters, so Conforte controlled nearly 20 percent of the votes.

Conforte made it his business to volunteer his two cents about candidates when he accompanied prostitutes to the polling place and visited Lockwood residents before elections with a bottle of whiskey under one arm and a turkey under the other: early "Christmas presents." Conforte fooled no one, said George. "But they [the tenants] were also paying him a mere thirty-five dollars a month in rent. And having Joe in your living room was such an honor, the people loved it." Besides, Conforte didn't try to hide his agenda. "I'm not going to lie to you," he once told a reporter. "I go around the trailer park and tell the people, 'Look you've got two candidates. Now I think this one is pro-prostitution, this one is not, and I would like you to vote for this one.' But where is the law against that?"

Conforte was finally brought down by the most commonplace of crimes: tax evasion. From the beginning, he had evaded paying taxes, soon attracting the IRS's attention and ultimately bogging down the courts with appeals of his convictions for tax evasion. When his appeals finally ran out, Conforte fled to Brazil to avoid imprisonment. He returned in 1983 as part of a federal plea bargain to testify against his former attorney, U.S. District Judge Harry Claiborne; Conforte claimed that Claiborne accepted an $85,000 bribe from him.

But Conforte's problems with the IRS weren't over. They came to a head in 1990 when he purposely defaulted on his monthly interest payments on the IRS's tax liability, and the IRS seized Mustang Ranch. The tax agency briefly considered running the brothel, but decided to sell it after the federal government became the butt of late-night television one-liners, with jokes poking fun at "Uncle Sam the pimp." When the property sold at auction for $1.49 million to a Victor Perry—who happened, not coincidentally, to be the brother of Conforte's personal lawyer—Conforte was hired as a consultant to oversee day-to-day operations. In 1991, he announced his retirement and once again fled the country to avoid further charges of tax evasion. (As of 2002, Conforte remains a fugitive, hiding out in South America. He even missed his wife Sally's funeral in 1993.)

But even as a fugitive, Conforte was by no means out of the picture. George received static-filled telephone calls from him at all hours; Conforte usually used a phone card and called from a pay phone to avoid having his exact whereabouts traced. Occasionally, George held the receiver up to my ear so I could hear Conforte's husky Mafioso-like voice ranting about the newest injustice obstructing his return to America. Mostly, Conforte wanted to hear news about Mustang. He also liked to huff and puff and bark orders for George and other old friends to carry out. When he was overtaxed by Conforte's incessant demands, George would avoid his calls for a couple of days.*

Conforte's exile came at a time when the industry was witnessing the emergence of a new breed of owners, more conventional businessmen who knew that political action contributions and lobbying efforts were all part of the game. But these new owners also posed dangers to the industry, as Conforte had once prophesied before his flight. When George first signed on as the brothels' lobbyist, Conforte took him aside to warn, "The one thing you've got to know is we've got a lot of squares getting into the business. They've got to understand that we're not selling cough drops, we're selling pussy. A lot of what works when you're selling cough drops doesn't work in our business." Still, neophytes could make a success.

Russ Reade was a case in point. A biology and sociology teacher at a small high school in northern California, Reade had burned out over his fifteen-year career, frustrated by the low pay and inadequate spending on department supplies. An advertisement in *The Wall Street Journal* in 1982, sandwiched between brokerage ads and stock quotes, attracted him and his business partner. It read: "Good cash flow, legal in Nevada."

*As executive director of the NBA, George was strictly a consultant and lobbyist. He has never been an employee of any individual brothel. Any attention George gave to Conforte's demands stemmed from their longstanding friendship.

All Reade knew about Nevada brothels came from a visit to Conforte's Wadsworth brothel in the early 1960s with a group of football players from the University of Nevada–Reno who were intent on recruiting Reade from Santa Rosa Junior College. "They wanted me to see some of the perks of living in Nevada. I was standoffish. I was too concerned about venereal disease. Condoms were not required then."

Reade and his partner spent six months doing research before buying the advertised brothel, the Chicken Ranch, for $1.25 million. (Today, brothel price tags vary from $200,000 to $4 million.) Although it was the closest brothel to Vegas, the Chicken Ranch was still a good distance away, fifty-five miles away, to be exact, outside the Nye County town of Pahrump. More remote than the Mustang, the Chicken Ranch drew fewer customers per day but made up for it because they were big spenders. The day I visited, women were turning one $1,000 trick after another. (Mustang parties averaged about $350.) The cab ride from Vegas alone cost over $200, so fewer barflies wasted prostitutes' time.

Reade's departure from teaching hadn't exactly been seamless. When he disclosed his intentions to colleagues—he had asked for a leave of absence, in case his new career didn't work out—the school board threatened to fire him and revoke his teaching certificate. His unusual career change made the *San Francisco Chronicle*, and the school superintendent became enraged and asked Reade what sort of role model he thought he was being for children. But Reade had always been a beloved teacher, and nearly two-thirds of the students signed a petition expressing their support. They presented it to the school board under the name "The Immoral Majority."

Sixteen years later, Reade was now fifty-eight years old, a fit man with salt-and-pepper hair and a Tom Selleck mustache; he still looked more like an all-American high school football star–turned–teacher than a brothel owner. He doubted whether any PTA would allow him to teach again, but he professed no regrets, having found an occupation that tripled his income.

Reade came to his new profession brimming with excitement and full of innovative ideas; he quickly proved himself to be cut from a different cloth than old-time brothel owners. Aware of the troubles Conforte and other owners had had with the IRS, Reade immediately sought counsel from first-rate accountants on how best to handle his finances in an aboveboard way. Unlike his predecessor, Walter Plankington—who, some rumored, kept two sets of books: one for the IRS, in which he reported annually grossing $150,000–$200,000, and one for himself, in which he recorded grossing $500,000–$1,000,000—Reade had every intention of keeping things legal. He brought in financial planners, tax counselors, and investment counselors to teach the prostitutes about tax planning and investment when he realized that less than 15 percent of them saved or invested any of their income. "I hope they can educate themselves and invest wisely so they can protect themselves past their prime years," said Reade. "I guess once a teacher, always a teacher."

Reade did admit to making some classic mistakes as a

novice. Brothel owners are infamous for taking advantage of their position and becoming involved with the women, generally without paying them. Although he initially resisted, Reade said, he gave in to temptation when some of the prostitutes took offense at his rebuffs. Because owner-prostitute relations were so common in the business, he said, Chicken Ranch prostitutes interpreted his refusal as a slight. Did Reade think he was better than they? After becoming involved with some of the women over the course of several months, Reade forced himself to go cold turkey because he realized that his behavior could cost him the respect of his staff as well as of other prostitutes.

When George approached the new Chicken Ranch owner to recruit him into the NBA, Reade jumped at the chance and even agreed to act as president. Still filled with the enthusiasm of a relative newcomer, he suggested to his colleagues that they hire a public relations firm. He hoped to market the brothels as legitimate businesses that contributed to Nevada's economic vitality and protected the public's health and safety. "I really tried to get all these renegade brothel operators to work together to protect the industry. The media constantly denigrated us, and nobody ever bothered to counter their arguments. When were we going to finally stand up and have official answers instead of no answers at all? We needed a nice, favorable report about the industry that we could send out anytime anybody called us up." When Reade proposed that each owner chip in $25,000 to cover a PR firm's fees, however, no one wanted to participate. Old-timers told him the brothels needed "to stay low in the bush." In the end, Reade and his partner alone financed the production of a polished information package, which they sent out to law enforcement officers, prosecutors, health agencies, and legislators.

But it was only a matter of time before Reade came to agree with other owners that it was better for the brothels to keep a low profile. After appearing on many call-in radio shows and television talk shows, from Dr. Ruth to *Donahue* and *Larry King Live*, in an effort to inform the public about Nevada's brothels, Reade finally accepted that these programs didn't care about facts, only sensation. "I thought that logically presenting what the brothels were about and what they accomplished would carry some weight and make points," said Reade. "But people had already made up their minds in the majority of cases and logic didn't crack the closed mind. People just wanted to be titillated. I decided to quit being a part of that because it didn't serve any purpose."

Today, Reade shies away from publicity. He wasn't even interested when George suggested that, given the pervasive, suggestive advertising of Vegas and Reno's strip joints and gentlemen's clubs, the NBA should challenge the ban on brothel advertising. He told George he didn't want to rock the legislative boat. Instead, Reade would continue his own discreet advertising campaign, which entailed educating Vegas cabdrivers about the health benefits of brothels in the hope that they would pass the information on to their passengers. He distributed to taxi drivers a flier entitled "Your Party Will Appreciate Knowing These Facts . . . ," which cited an

Associated Press article about the absence of HIV infection in the brothels. Finally, Reade pushed Chicken Ranch souvenirs, giving women a commission for selling their customers brothel T-shirts and other mementos. "The girls make more than I do. But the whole idea is to get the shirts out there without ruffling too many feathers in the process."

In contrast, Dennis Hof didn't care how many feathers he ruffled with his publicity stunts. Hof, fifty-three, a former condominium time-share developer and brothel customer, owns two brothels in Lyon County, Moonlite Bunny Ranch and Miss Kitty's. He has been in the business a little more than seven years but has already gained notoriety on par with Conforte's. In January 1998, he hired John Wayne Bobbitt, of severed-penis fame, to tend bar at the Moonlite and drive its limousine. That same year, he began hiring porn stars like Sunset Thomas, Samantha Strong, and Laurie Holmes as brothel prostitutes, with minimums of $1,000. Hof's newest PR concept was to film XXX-rated films on location at the Moonlite. He also had plans to add a 100,000-square-foot adult bookstore and go in on an Internet venture with *Hustler* magazine mogul Larry Flynt.

According to George Flint, owners like Hof, who wanted to mass-market the brothels, threatened the entire industry. "You're witnessing the fragmentation of the Brothel Association as it's been," he told me the day he learned Hof had blitzed the media, from *Hard Copy* to *The Howard Stern Show*, with boasts that his business had improved 20 percent because of Viagra. "Dennis Hof is a very aggressive businessman and promoter, and very naïve about the tenuousness of the business and the required delicacy of handling certain things. Leave the industry up to owners like Dennis Hof and you won't have any organization or industry in eight years." Because the NBA didn't serve as a governing organization, brothel owners were free to operate their businesses as they liked. George could only sit them down and advise them to try to remain discreet. Up to that point, he had been unsuccessful with Hof.

George hoped to have better luck with two of Nevada's newest brothel owners, Mack and Angel Moore. A former mortician from Oregon, Mack relocated to southern Nevada with his second wife, Angel, to try his hand at running a brothel. They had bought Fran's Star Ranch, which sat on seventy-seven acres of farmland in Beatty. Mack aspired to cultivate fruits, vegetables, and a new sort of brothel business. They renamed the place after Angel: Angel's Ladies Brothel. In contrast to Mustang Ranch, it was a mom-and-pop operation in the desert, offering a lineup of no more than five women. Like the parlors in many of Nevada's smaller brothels, Angel's Ladies felt like a cramped living room in a prefab home. Acquainted with the business as an occasional customer because of his first wife's alleged frigidity, Mack was feverish with new-fangled ideas.

Devout Christians, Mack and Angel required everyone (including any customers who happened to visit around six P.M.) to participate in a sit-down dinner each evening, with a fine imposed on anyone who started eating before grace was said. The brothel was dry, and it was the first to institute random drug testing of its workers. Other owners doubted that Mack and Angel would be able to attract enough women to work under these conditions. (Mack and Angel hoped to compensate by offering a 55–45 cut in favor of prostitutes, rather than the usual 50–50 cut.) Of more concern, perhaps, was the fact that Angel had been lining up, competing with the working girls, allegedly "only when there weren't enough girls on the floor." When I went out for a visit, I found a photo album entitled "Angel's Services" sitting on a table in the parlor. In it were photos of Angel in a variety of sexual positions with Mack and other men.

Angel felt strongly that if a man came in and bought forty-five minutes' worth of sex, he should get a party for that long, whether the woman got him off faster or not. "Sex is a beautiful thing God gave us to release the tension inside. Sex is more than money; it's taking care of the individual." Angel claimed she wasn't taking business away from the girls and really only dated clients no one else wanted. "But I don't want someone to walk outside and hang himself because he couldn't relieve himself." Mack said he didn't mind since he and Angel were swingers anyway, but the women did. Angel was stealing their customers, they felt, and because she was the owner, they had no recourse. George still hoped he could educate these amateurs and get them in line.

Still, no matter how hard brothel owners like Russ Reade, Dennis Hof, and even Mack and Angel Moore tried to normalize the business, through mass marketing or proselytizing teetotalism, the results were mixed. In the face of Nevada's "don't ask, don't tell" attitude, most brothel owners and employees coped by keeping low public profiles and insulating themselves within the business. The few outsiders adopted into this world became fiercely loyal and protective. What developed was an insular subculture kept on the fringes of mainstream society.

8 .. AN EXTENDED FAMILY

I often saw just how close-knit the brothel community was. That community extended beyond the prostitutes themselves; if anything, the other employees were more protective of the women than they were of each other. To be an employee at a brothel—a floor maid, bartender, cook, laundry maid, whatever—inevitably meant tolerating derogatory comments about the sort of women who would do "that." One developed a tough skin.

One afternoon, for example, I overheard a customer sitting alone at the bar, hunched over his third Jack Daniel's on the rocks, hiss, "Psst. Hey, bartender. Which of these bitches would you fuck?"

Brian, the day bartender at Mustang #1, was working.

He looked up from the sink where he stood rinsing beer glasses, cocked his head, and furrowed his eyebrows. "Excuse me," he said, just barely concealing his hostility. "What did you say?"

Too drunk to recognize his bad manners, the customer repeated himself. "Which of these bitches is worth my money?"

Brian's ruddy Irish face turned crimson. "Let's get something straight, asshole," he snapped. "These are not bitches, these are my friends. This may be a legal brothel, but at least you don't waste your money buying a girl fourteen drinks with no promise of getting laid. Here, the ladies are straight up. You don't have to buy them a drink, and you're guaranteed a lay. You treat these women with respect or I'm going to bounce your ass right out of here."

The man sat stunned. Under his breath, he mumbled an apology before slipping off his bar stool to head to the men's room.

By the time the man returned, word had spread among the working girls there was a jerk in the bar. For the rest of the afternoon, every prostitute he propositioned "walked" him, deliberately quoting a prohibitively high price. They trusted that Blanche the floor maid would excuse them: a former brothel prostitute herself, Blanche knew all about partying with men who didn't respect working girls.

When the customer finally left, as sexually unsatisfied as he came in and much more frustrated, I asked Brian about the confrontation. Fortunately, he said, customers like that were few and far between. Outside, however, Brian heard his fair share of disparaging comments about brothel prostitutes, and he was just as quick to jump to the women's defense.

Brian had never expected to become a defender of Mustang Ranch prostitutes. He had stumbled upon the job: working as a security guard at a nearby casino, he met a Mustang Ranch bartender who told him of the opening. Brian had found the salary increase and the schedule—one week on, one week off—more attractive than the fact that he would be working in a brothel. A "burnt-out" forty-nine-year-old ex-cop from California, Brian had no romantic visions of prostitution: "I'd had my fill of drug-crazed girls covered with sores, stoned or smashed out of their minds, propositioning me at the window of my patrol car."

Despite himself, Brian had come to see the women less as degenerates and more as human beings in the two and a half years he worked at Mustang. He knew that some of the prostitutes abused drugs and alcohol, he said, but he respected the fact that the women sold sex as licensed professionals rather than as illicit hustlers. "I no longer feel prostitution is a moral issue or a question of someone's integrity and principles," he said. "I think it's just a job to a lot of girls. I come and do my job tending bar, and they do theirs. And least they're doing it responsibly and respectably."

Instead of pitying the women, Brian had come to feel genuine empathy for them. He enjoyed listening to their troubles and giving advice. Flattered by their trust, Brian reciprocated with unwavering loyalty. "I [couldn't] give a shit whether I make some guy a Bacardi and Coke correctly or not. I give a damn about the women. Frankly, they're all I give a damn about here. It took a lot for them to trust me. They figured I was just another bartender who wouldn't last six months before getting canned for trying to get into one of the girls' pants."

Although Mustang rules prohibited employees from "fraternizing" with brothel prostitutes, all too frequently staff members assumed that employment entitled them to freebies, or at least discounts. (To confuse the message, George Flint did occasionally give male employees free passes as bonuses, but he expected them to be used at other brothels.) For many years, to prevent consorting, brothels wouldn't hire men. Male owners were supposed to stay behind the scenes, leaving day-to-day operations to the female staff. Today, men are permitted to work more visibly—as cooks, bartenders, cashiers, and maintenance people—but women still hold all the managerial and floor maid positions.

But Brian hadn't faltered. Having been divorced after eighteen years of marriage, he was committed to being faithful to his live-in girlfriend of almost four years. Despite Brian's protestations, his male friends and the men he served in the bar kept fantasizing about all the free sex they thought came with brothel employment.

Not every employee was as carefully chaste as Brian. There was Jeffrey, for example, another bartender, a big burly man who looked not unlike Popeye's nemesis, Bluto. Jeffrey was Mustang's resident bad boy, and with his long sleek ponytail, goatee, and Harley-Davidson, he did nothing to negate the image. He let it be known that he had ridden briefly with the Hell's Angels. Jeffrey came from a long line of Mustang old-timers, among them his father, Joe Conforte's former bodyguard and right-hand man and one of only two employees to be given a lifetime pension for his years of service. Jeffrey had tended bar and provided security at Mustang since he was twenty. Now in his thirties, he was nearly a Mustang institution in his own right.

Jeffrey felt entitled to ignore brothel rules, and he had amassed a history of dalliances with working girls, sometimes seeing several women simultaneously. It wasn't unusual for women to buy him expensive gifts in order to win his attention and affection. Rumor had it that Jeffrey wasn't beyond getting Mustang prostitutes to pay *him* to have sex. "He's very protective, and that's seductive," explained one woman. "When a guy gets out of line with one of us and we hit the panic button, Jeffrey usually gets there first, even before security. I think a lot of the girls become infatuated with him, wishing they had somebody like that with them all the time."

Curiously, the women felt very little ill will toward Jeffrey, despite the numerous hearts he'd broken. I never heard a bad word said about him, and I heard plenty of dirt dished on other brothel staff. Most of the working girls felt indebted to him and consequently were very loyal. One working girl would only say, "Me and Jeffrey go back a long ways. I would kill for him. Actually, I'd rather not talk too much about Jeffrey without him here."

I got to see Jeffrey in action as soon as Heather appeared on the scene. He strutted past her with his chest puffed out, pretending not to see her, for the first few days. After almost a week, he began honoring her with an occasional glance or grunt when he served her drinks. Then one morning I caught the two of them cozying up to each other at the bar. Without much persuasion, Jeffrey had gotten Heather to pull out two porn magazines with back-page advertisements for the Houston "modeling agency" where she used to work. Coyly, Heather flipped the pages, showing off the ads that featured her dressed provocatively with a cartoon bubble over her head saying, "I speak Greek." Heather explained that meant she performed anal intercourse.

After their tête-à-tête, Heather placed eight dollars on the bar and seductively mouthed a thank-you before she turned to join the morning's first lineup. Jeffrey grinned devilishly, obviously pleased. Brothel patrons were notoriously unappreciative of bartenders, who were left to rely on the generosity and good fortune of the working girls on busy days. Before Heather's tip, Jeffrey had only made $33 in tips since starting his shift six hours earlier, at two A.M.

The next thing I knew, Heather started blowing off our daily runs. The first time it happened, she said she had gone running earlier in the morning with Sheba, the brothel dog. The next morning, when I went to scratch at her door (the women preferred scratching to knocking), she didn't answer. When I asked Blanche, the floor maid, if she knew where Heather was, she said Heather had already left to go running. At first, I was perplexed. We had been running with such regularity; why would she suddenly snub me? But all became clear when I confronted her and she said that instead of running the paved road past the neighboring Peri brothers' farm, she had been running up the dirt road behind the brothel, "past Jeffrey's trailer." (A number of brothel staff members rented trailers from the brothel and lived on this dirt road.) So Heather was sneaking over to Jeffrey's place each morning. I wondered how her boyfriend, who was back home in Texas minding her two daughters, would feel about this.

A few days later, Heather wanted to recommence our morning jog. I asked her if anything was going on between her and Jeffrey. She blushed and said they were just friends. She did volunteer that she went up regularly to Jeffrey's trailer to visit, but nothing physical had happened. I volunteered, in kind, that I thought Jeffrey was hot. Guiltily, she blushed again.

Jeffrey wasn't the only staff member to defy brothel rules and get involved with the women. Most other men got burned in the process, however. Sally Conforte used to warn her employees to save themselves the heartache and "not fuck her girls." For some men, pain came from watching their love interests seduce countless other men. Others were disappointed when their illusions of the women as ideal mates were shattered by reality. "You can't help but get jaded," Brian said. "When people ask me if I like working in a brothel, I say, 'Sure, if you like working around fifty-four girls with multiple personalities who are all on the rag at the same time.' "

In truth, working for the women of Mustang Ranch *was* tough, but the employees generally appreciated how demanding the women's work was, and knew the women relied on them for protection. The staff's stewardship did not go unrecognized. Once employees were considered dependable and trustworthy, women acknowledged their efforts with extra tips. On their birthdays, they got cards signed by the working girls, who also contributed cash. And when catastrophe befell an employee, the brothel community rallied in a show of support. When a fire left a Mustang kitchen assistant named Kent, his wife, and their three children homeless, the women took up a collection that amounted to several thousand dollars. A Mustang employee for less than two years, Kent wept when he opened the envelope.

For many employees, Mustang was a home away from home. Although they did not live on the premises, many of them seemed as if they did. Mark, a parlor helper, told me, "I basically live at Mustang. I don't need to go anywhere else. I get my three square meals here and even after work I hang out in the bar because I love the people." Forty-five-year-old Miyuki had been a Mustang laundry maid for over eighteen years but confessed that she was still embarrassed whenever she overheard the working girls discussing their parties with customers. She tried to avoid coming face-to-face with clients, instead staying in the laundry room where a colossal washer and dryer churned away all day and night. But Miyuki's discomfort did not make her feel less a member of the community. Her husband, a Mustang security guard, had died twelve years earlier in a traffic accident, and Mustang was all she had. "My family all in Japan, so I don't have nobody in America," said Miyuki. "The people here—the girls, the employees, the management—help me keep going. That's why I make it. Here it's like home to me. On my week off, I stop by just to visit, just to say hi."

Even the suppliers who came out to Mustang became part of the community; most of them found a role for themselves beyond peddling their goods and services. At first, I had been surprised to learn that an entire industry existed to capitalize on these women. On my first visit I had wondered where the women purchased their dizzying array of bodysuits, slip dresses, and lingerie, all in a rainbow of vivid colors—fuchsia, cherry-red, turquoise, neon green, jet-black, and virginal white. Were these mail-order clothes, or did women shop for them openly in the outside world? Neither, I soon learned; the women were serviced by specialty clothing vendors.

Door-to-door salespeople were a long-standing tradition in Nevada's legal houses of prostitution. The market was ideal: women living in confinement, making considerable cash daily with no place to spend it. As a brothel clothing vendor named Leo put it, "What we have here is a captive audience, a *very* captive audience. I like a captive audience." And so he should. George Flint estimated that brothel prostitutes statewide spent a minimum of $350,000 annually on vendors' merchandise. At Mustang Ranch alone, women bought approximately $150,000 worth of goods each year.

Leo was sixty-nine and had been selling clothing in Nevada's legal brothels for over twenty years. Before being allowed inside and being accepted as a member of the vendor corps, however, Leo had had to earn his customers' trust. "For years, brothel prostitutes from the Chicken Ranch came into my Vegas boutique," Leo said. "Vegas only had conventional, wholesome dress shops. Mine was the only boutique that sold long, slinky dresses, clothes a hooker could wear. They got to know me and to trust me. Only then did they finally persuade Walter [the former owner of the Chicken Ranch] to let me inside the brothel. It was easier for me to go out to them than for them to come seventy miles to me."

Leo eventually sold his shop and renovated a retired Greyhound bus into a traveling boutique, with hundreds of garments hanging from clothing racks on both sides of the aisle and a dressing room in back. Leo visited more than twenty brothels a month; his Greyhound had over 500,000 miles on it. Every Saturday morning, he came out to Mustang and set up temporary shop in the kitchen, where he hung his goods on portable racks. The clothes came mostly from the manufacturers that supplied mail-order companies with names like Steamed Heat International and International Dancing. Leo cut the labels out of all his outfits in order to keep his five main competitors—up from two or three when he first started selling at Mustang—from muscling in on his turf and selling the same merchandise.

As brothel minimums had risen over the years, so had Leo's prices. Twenty years ago, when the house minimum was $20, his dresses sold for $35 apiece. Now dress prices ran between $80 and $150. "A girl who spends money makes money," Leo always lectured to the women as they looked over his clothes. "If you look like a two-thousand-dollar hooker, men will pay you two thousand dollars. If you look like a sixty-dollar whore, you'll only make sixty dollars."

Leo missed the days of old, when management forced women to invest in their wardrobes, buying evening gowns, furs, and precious stones. "Sally Conforte was very smart," Leo soliloquized. "She was a nut for the glitzy and shiny. Sally built an empire on this image. When Sally walked around, girls shook and shivered. God forbid they didn't have a sequin on their dress. With Sally no longer in the picture, girls today don't spend money on clothes. And let me tell you, it's reflected in the money they make—five hundred, six hundred a day now as opposed to a thousand to two thousand a day in the past."

The first time I met Leo, he was muttering about Reno's upcoming Rodeo Days, the one week of the year when Mustang prostitutes were permitted to dress down in sloppy denim jeans, T-shirts, cowboy boots, and hats. In his opinion, however, rodeo cowboys didn't want to see women unkempt. Filthy from lassoing broncos all afternoon, these men wanted to see spruced-up women in sexy attire. But no one seemed to pay Leo much mind. The next week, the women gleefully swapped their mini-dresses and lingerie for Levi's and men's white cotton T-shirts.

Luckily for Leo, the women displaced a lot of their anxieties and insecurities about work onto their clothes, blaming their outfits when customers failed to pick them. If they were having a bad night, women often changed their clothes repeatedly, sometimes fifteen times.

Over time, I would learn that even though Leo liked to lecture and give the women an earful, he felt very protective of them. Over the years, he had become a fixture at Mustang, which, more than any other brothel, he considered a surrogate home. Leo even lived, like much of the staff, in the Mustang-owned Lockwood Mobile Home Park, and he frequently dropped in during the week to visit with friends. His fourth wife (of five) was a brothel prostitute to whom he'd sold merchandise.

When I saw the vendors' clothing racks from a distance, I couldn't help imagining myself in various risqué outfits. I had always been intrigued by lingerie, even if my own drawers were full of cotton briefs and sports bras. But I'd certainly never seen outfits the likes of which I saw at Mustang Ranch.

One Saturday morning near the end of one of my visits, Leo had just unloaded his Greyhound bus and was arranging his merchandise for display. Heather, my running mate, was aimlessly sifting through a rack of new dresses. I walked over to her and peered over her shoulder. When Leo spotted me hovering, he sidled up to the two of us. "I only have stuff for working girls," he said. Before either Heather or I could respond, Tanya, the Mustang veteran, sitting at a nearby table, interjected, "When she's here with us, she's just like a working girl." Leo didn't say anything, but he let it alone and walked away.

I began looking over Leo's clothes. Leo interrupted to ask, with the cool disdain of a salesclerk on Rodeo Drive, how he could help me. "I'm thinking of buying an outfit to take home with me, for my husband," I said, surprising myself.

Apparently he didn't believe me, for he shook his head and mumbled something about my needing to buy some nice lingerie in town.

Heather squealed and held up a red Lycra peignoir trimmed with lush marabou feathers. There was one lone hook to fasten between the breasts. "Oooooh," she crooned, "try this one on. It's so sexy." I had to admit it was. Heather asked Leo if I could try on the peignoir. He nodded, but grunted that he doubted it would fit me properly.

I followed Heather back to the Jacuzzi room with its walls of full-length mirrors, and stripped down. While I had no trouble slipping into the red robe, I thought I had my panties on wrong. Why were my buttocks hanging out? I wasn't *that* big, was I? Heather noticed my difficulty and gave the panties a yank. They settled into place. "There," she said. "Much better."

"Ohhhh. It's a G-string," I said sheepishly.

By now, a few other working girls had come back to watch the show, including Brittany. "I'm liking the red," she said. The rest of the women nodded in agreement. I looked in the mirror: Huh, not half-bad. It was easy to lose perspective about standards of physical beauty in a brothel, surrounded by women who'd made major investments in cosmetic surgery from breast augmentations and tummy tucks to face-lifts and liposuction. Baby had spent over $20,000 on body improvements, including breast implants, rhinoplasty, lip implants, dental bonding, tattoos, and piercing of her right nipple. Women often debated how much cosmetic surgery actually improved a prostitute's business. The women insisted I buy the peignoir to give my husband a thrill. Heather suggested I offer Leo $75 (it was tagged at $95). He accepted. "You've got fine taste in fashion," he said obsequiously.

Another vendor who'd earned a special place in the hearts of the women of Mustang Ranch was Chau, the manicurist. A Vietnamese woman in her forties, Chau had been coming out to Mustang for almost five years and took her responsibilities very seriously. "She builds her schedule around ours," said an appreciative prostitute named Autumn as Chau finished applying a second coat of burgundy acrylic to her nails. We were in Mustang's makeshift beauty shop, which was equipped with a shampoo sink, overhead dryer, stylist chair, and manicure station. Photographs of "with it" hairdos dating back to the early 1980s decorated the walls.

Chau visited Mustang every Sunday morning and frequently stuck around until the small hours of Monday to make sure prostitutes on all shifts had the chance to get their nails done. Her decision to provide services to brothel prostitutes had not come easily. When Chau's community first learned of her plans to sell manicures at Mustang Ranch, she faced serious pressure to give up the idea. "At first I was scared, because my people—my Vietnamese people—say how terrible it is here, how mean the people are," said Chau in a soft voice. "My people say if they [brothel management] don't have enough girls, they make me work, too."

Chau quickly discovered the women weren't monsters and made the decision to extend herself beyond the usual responsibilities of a manicurist. "Nail lady very important lady because you have to talk with your customers," Chau explained. "Everybody sometimes needs to talk, even these girls. I give them my home phone number and tell them to call even after midnight." In addition, Chau offered to provide an alibi: "The girls tell me how hard it is when their family wants to know where they work or their kids want to come visit," she said, tears welling up in her eyes. "I let them use my address and phone number. I take the messages and I tell them to call home."

Mustang gave Chau a sense of purpose and filled a void in her life. "My parents got killed by the Communists when I was three and a half years old," she said, her cheery veneer punctured as tears streamed down her cheeks. "All my life I look for family, for love. The girls out here, they're family to me. When I have a bad time, have a hard day, they come and give me a hug. I come to work late, they call me at home and want to know if I'm okay. When I work late, they ask me if I want a room to sleep here. The girls say 'Chau is family.' That's why I come out here to work. I need them."

Even a few regular customers had managed to carve out a place for themselves within Mustang's community. The most conspicuous was Frankie, a large thirty-three-year-old Samoan man with a stocky wrestler's build who had been patronizing Nevada's brothels for more than half his life. At fifteen, he rode his dirt bike to one of the Carson City brothels to lose his virginity. Since "becoming a man," Frankie figured he had spent over $100,000, averaging three or four parties per week with brothel prostitutes. "It's real hard for me to stay away for more than two or three days, unless I have something else to do on the outside," he told me one day.

It was this compulsion that prompted him to dream up a job that enabled him to spend almost six days a week brothel-hopping. His business? A jukebox repair company that serviced the Reno and Carson City brothels exclusively. Now Frankie was no longer just another customer. He had earned a place in the women's hearts, along with the affectionate nickname Jukebox Frankie. "The girls depend on me to keep the CDs up-to-date and sizzling," he said, grinning from ear to ear. Frankie's novel enterprise was also the perfect way to explain to his wife of fourteen years the inordinate amount of time he spent at the Ranches. Frankie even went so far as to write off his weekly "parties" as business expenses. "I put a lot of my money back into the house," he said. "I believe it's always good to do business with the people who do business with you."

Among the women, Frankie had earned a title long before he started fixing jukeboxes. Frankie was considered a "professional trick." Professional tricks differed from regular customers in that they prided themselves on having mastered the ropes of the business. Most were lonely single men with few sexual outlets. The brothels offered them more than sex; they gave them a community of which the men could feel a part. In fact, the brothels typically became these men's primary social circles, with many befriending each other, making excursions to the brothels together, and spending countless hours talking about which women they had been with and how much time they'd received.

Fifty-year-old Stewart, an overweight computer salesman, was a case in point. Originally from Huntington Beach, California, Stewart made his first visit to Mustang Ranch back in 1978, when he "went crazy and did sixteen girls in four days." Tickled pink, he pledged to visit the brothel every chance he got, sometimes "vacationing" alone there as many as six times a year despite his relatively new marriage. Finally, in 1984, Stewart divorced his wife and relocated to Reno, solely to be closer to the brothels. Now he and his cronies, Roger and Tom, haunted the brothel, visiting an average of five times a week. Like yentas, these three men prattled on daily over the telephone and in person about their mutual obsession. Said Stewart, who habitually wore a gold chain necklace with a dollar-sign pendant, and a matching money pin on the breast pocket of his shirt, "We talk amongst ourselves all the time. If we get a real good one [prostitute], everybody's gonna hear about it. If it's a terrible one, everybody's gonna hear about that too."

All three men believed themselves to be special favorites with brothel insiders. A bachelor in his early forties, with curly salt-and-pepper hair down to his shoulders like an aging rock star, Roger saw Mustang "like a second home" over the course of his twelve-year patronage. "I walk in here and I'm well known. When I come in about eight o'clock, the bartender immediately sets me up, already knows what I like. The girls are accustomed to me; they say hello and all know my name. The girls aren't really prostitutes to me anymore. They're more like friends. It's like walking into a local bar, like Cheers."

In reality, however, most of the women had a love-hate relationship with professional tricks like Roger and Stewart. While they depended on such men for regular business, the working girls generally resented their cockiness and vocal knowledge of brothel protocol. One professional trick brought his own egg timer to make sure he got the time he'd paid for. Professional tricks were also notorious for trying to take advantage of the less knowledgeable, the new turn-outs, who could often be conned into giving customers top-of-the-line parties for a bargain rate.

The professional tricks were smug because they knew that if a party was unsatisfactory, the client could complain to management and receive restitution, despite the woman's independent-contractor status. When professional tricks complained that a woman had charged too much, stiffed them on time, or even been bitchy, Mustang management's response was that the customer was always right. "I know what the prices run," Stewart said. "If a girl gets out of line, I just tell the floor maid. She'll inform the girl, 'Stewart's a very good customer and he better come out smiling or you can just pack your bags right now.' If the girl doesn't treat me right during a party, the floor maid may ask if I want to pick another girl, or she may refund half the money I spent, docking it from the girl's books. Management doesn't want to lose a regular like me."

He was right about that. Stewart spent $30,000 to $40,000 a year on parties at Mustang. That sum gave me new appreciation for what his regularity as a customer meant to the women and the industry. In recognition of his loyal patronage, Mustang management agreed to sell Stewart $3,000 worth of passes for $2,000, which he split up among his friends.

Stewart, Roger, and Tom were a constant presence at the brothel. I imagined I would be hard-pressed to find any other outsiders more obsessed with this subculture than they were. Needless to say, I was wrong. I found just such a group on that great and universal haven for obsessed loners, the Internet.

9 .. BROTHEL.COM

With the elegance of a soap opera starlet at the Emmy Awards, Annabella rose as her name was announced. Forty-six pairs of eyes in a banquet room, mine among them, followed the tall, statuesque beauty as she strode to the front of the room to collect her prize: a five-inch-by-four-inch object made of clear glass cut in the shape of a diamond with a plaque fixed to its base that bore her name and the words COURTESAN OF THE YEAR.

Described by her admirers as a cross between Christie Brinkley and Lisa Kudrow, Annabella had worked as a model, posing for porn magazines, before becoming a brothel prostitute. Of half–American Indian and half-Irish descent, she had large gray eyes, a sparkling smile, and thick blond hair that cascaded down her back. She wore a shimmery gold lamé gown that would have made the late Sally Conforte green with envy, especially because Annabella worked at one of Mustang Ranch's biggest competitors, the Sagebrush, located in Carson City.

I had never met Annabella before that night, but I had heard about her. Customers and former Sagebrush prostitutes who had moved over to Mustang Ranch spoke in awed tones not only of her beauty but of her lengthy and extraordinary parties. Men routinely compared her talents to those of a gifted psychic or therapist, describing her as intuitively alert to the sort of woman each man wanted her to be and then somehow capable of becoming that woman. "She is totally service-oriented," one client told me. "She gets completely into your mind, body, and soul. You are her world for the duration of the party." Annabella was also known to be pricey. Rumor had it that a "straight lay" with her typically cost $1,100.

Annabella seemed genuinely appreciative of the award. "Thank you all so very much," she said demurely. During the standing ovation that followed, she discreetly tried to dab away the tears welling up in the corners of her eyes.

It was late July 1998, and I had found myself a guest at the second annual CyberWhoreMonger Convention, a gathering of forty-some men and a handful of prostitutes who communicated by way of a customer-designed website—the Georgia Powers Bordello Connection—devoted to their shared obsession, Nevada's licensed brothels. The men were a motley crew straight out of the ballroom scene in *The Rocky Horror Picture Show*—an assortment of dementedly exuberant men of all shapes and ages, most with glasses and giddy smiles on their faces. Until tonight, most of the guests had never laid eyes on one another and only knew each other by their computer pseudonyms.

As guests first entered the private room at the restaurant, Reno's Famous Murphy's, event organizers handed them a laminated card that read: "The bearer of this card is a member of that group known as the CyberWhoreMongers. Membership in this group signifies that this person is of low moral character, is known to consort with disreputable companions and spend his money foolishly." The card certifying membership had been issued by the Chief CyberWhoreMonger, who went by the handle Bashful and who happened to be my date for the evening.

I had had only brief contact with Bashful before the convention. Several years earlier, he had contacted me by e-mail to ask if he could post my condom breakage study on his website, to inform men of the results. Through the grapevine, he learned that I was back at Mustang and once again e-mailed me to invite me to be his date for the convention. Curious, I accepted.

Bashful picked me up at Mustang before the convention in a caramel-colored GMC truck with out-of-state plates. I was to discover that he was deeply proud of knowing all there was to know about Nevada's brothels, and he pumped me about my experiences at Mustang. I, in turn, learned that Bashful was thirty-nine, that he worked as a computer programmer for the U.S. military, and that he was eager to share his version of the tale of the origins of the Internet's first website dedicated to legalized prostitution.

Bashful first learned of Nevada's brothels in 1985, when, as an undergraduate physics major, he overheard one of the graduate students bragging about his summer sexual escapades there. Bashful sought out a book devoted to the subject, Gerald Paine's *A Bachelor's Guide to the Brothels of Nevada*, the forerunner of J. R. Schwartz's *Official Guide to the Best Cat Houses in Nevada*. (Written by enthusiastic customers, both are quippy, subjective guidebooks for other men.) At the time, Bashful was still a virgin. "I never had any girlfriends, no women at all. I always put it off. I always thought that when I went to college I was going to win the Nobel Prize in physics and marry a movie star. Then I realized that I wasn't a very good physicist and got into computers. I figured that someday I would worry about getting a girlfriend. The fact is I just put everything off."

Including losing weight. Bashful had always been overweight, and now he weighed over three hundred pounds. An immense man with a full beard, he resembled a lumbering bear. But beneath his thick, functional wire-rimmed glasses, his eyes betrayed a vulnerability and shy charm. Bashful's procrastination in pursuing intimate sexual relationships was intricately linked with his procrastination in losing weight. "It's like the Groucho Marx line: I would never join a club that would have me. I wouldn't want a woman who would want a large mammal such as myself."

Bashful did lose some weight—one of two times in his life that he got down to 190 pounds—before he first ventured out to the brothels, intent on losing his virginity. It was May 1986, a month shy of his twenty-seventh birthday. "When I got to Mustang, there was a huge lineup of girls, and the bar area was jam-packed with guys. The hostess asked if I would like to pick a lady. The place was silent, everyone was looking at me. I picked a girl on the far left who seemed to be a little bigger-busted than normal, and had a fairly nice figure. Then—and nothing like this has ever happened since—all the guys in the bar started cheering. In my mind, I could see hats flying up in the air as they cheered, but I doubt that happened. She was a real nice girl, and I had a real nice evening. I still remember driving back to Reno afterwards, it was such a sense of ela-tion. It was just wonderful. It was truly more than I had expected."

But the loss of his virginity didn't encourage Bashful to try his luck with dating or to slim down. Instead, he became pre-occupied with the brothels, making trips out to Nevada twice a year. "I became addicted, obsessed, maybe more than I should have. It was just too easy." Bashful kept his semiannual brothel migrations secret until 1994; he was then a graduate student in electrical engineering, enrolled in digital processing and filtering classes. He had begun surfing the Internet and stumbled across the alt.sex.services Usenet newsgroup, a bul-letin board devoted to sex-related material. Here, much to his surprise, he found two items pertaining to Nevada's legal brothels: Blake Wilfong's "Unofficial Chicken Ranch FAQ" and a message posted by a man about a girl named Jennifer at the Cherry Patch II brothel.

First posted in October 1994 by a computer scientist who

had worked as a consultant to NASA, the "Unofficial Chicken Ranch FAQ" was meant to "make information about the Chicken Ranch more widely available to men who might wish to go there." Wilfong claimed he had no affiliation with the brothel, apart from being a customer for over eight years. The website detailed the legality, regulation, and safety of the Chicken Ranch and offered Wilfong's testimonial that "after approximately one hundred parties with thirty-three ladies at the Chicken Ranch over a period of eight years, I have never contracted an STD."

Wilfong gave readers a slew of suggestions, ranging from advice on transportation to and from the brothel, to the best hours to visit. He even offered a tip on how to handle the tricky task of remembering women's names during lineup: "Don't feel bad; most customers can't remember all the ladies' names. It's fine to say 'the second from the right' or 'the lady in the blue dress.' But here is a way you can easily name the lady you want: As the first lady comes out and introduces herself, memorize her name. Now, as the second lady introduces herself, decide whether you'd rather party with her or the first lady. If you want to party with the second lady, forget about the first lady and memorize the second lady's name. Continue this process as the lineup forms. This way, you only have to remember one name, the name of the most attractive lady you have seen so far."

Wilfong's candid and public admission to being a trick surprised Bashful. But he was even more astonished by the second item posted, the message about Jennifer at the Cherry Patch II. "Frankly, it was far more explicit than anything I was interested in. He talked about fisting her and all. I was thinking, God I can't believe that this is on the Internet. But he claimed that she wanted it out there, on the Internet, and that she was getting customers from it. He was apparently getting a lot of e-mail from guys who wanted to know more about the brothels and prostitution in general. Finding these two documents had a big effect on me. For the very first time, I realized just how powerful a medium the Internet could be."

Inspired by both men's outspokenness as well as by Gerald Paine and J. R. Schwartz's guidebooks, Bashful set out to engineer a cyberspace guide for consumers to Nevada's legal brothels. In November 1994, Bashful first posted to alt.sex.services a text file with questions he thought people might have about the brothels and his best answers. "I was nervous. I thought the FBI was going to bust down my front door and arrest me that next morning on pandering charges or some such nonsense. I thought maybe people were tracing me somehow. But it's never been a problem." Within hours, Bashful had received a response from a man who said he had visited a number of the brothels and preferred the smaller houses. This man also informed Bashful of the double-buzz trick— ringing the doorbell twice, the signal created by the brothels for nonclients to use upon arrival at the outside gate—to avoid getting a lineup, which Bashful ended up including in his FAQ. "That's one thing that guys really dig. They love the double-buzz trick, because they don't want to see a lineup. They just want to go in, settle down, look around, and take their time."

While similar to Wilfong's FAQ in many ways, Bashful's "Frequently Asked Questions on Legal Prostitution in Nevada" differed in others. For one thing, Bashful mentioned some of Nevada's other brothels, not only Wilfong's beloved Chicken Ranch. Perhaps the single biggest difference, however, was Bashful's inclusion of a recommendation of a specific working girl: Baby, from Mustang Ranch. "It just seemed like a naughty and fun thing to do. In all my years visiting brothels, it was very rare that I would see the same girl again because of their high turnover rate. But I had managed to catch Baby at the Mustang Ranch for about three or four in a row. Plus, she was my favorite, and I thought maybe this would impress the girl that I loved."

Following Bashful's example, men began e-mailing him their endorsements of other brothel prostitutes. "For the first year, I would only allow messages about Baby. If I didn't know the girl personally, why would I want to stick my neck out and take the chance that some guy would blame me for not having a good time with her? Why would I stake my professional reputation on it?" Eventually, however, Bashful acceded, inaugurating his first collection of "field reports." More than 400 field reports on more than 150 prostitutes from twenty-two brothels have been made available, all of them indexed by woman, brothel, date of posting, and author, like the *Zagat Survey* restaurant guide.

While most reports included men's overall impressions of paid sex with an individual prostitute, they refrained from describing the sex acts graphically or in excruciating detail. Still others read like masturbatory fantasies from the pages of *Penthouse*. "She promptly mounted me, sliding a very TIGHT (and I want to emphasize TIGHT) pussy around my hard-on. . . .

She used her muscles to extract every last drop of cum from my once hard-on that was growing ever increasingly limp." Feeling protective of the women I had come to know, I found these types of reviews insulting; the descriptions reduced the women to sex objects stripped of their humanity. Like boastful adolescent boys, they congratulated themselves on their sexual prowess and talent. "She started to move back and forth, letting out little moans of pleasure which I think were actually real." It was just that—the opportunity to posture and brag—that Web users delighted in most, according to Bashful. "It makes you immortal! My ego is saying, A thousand years from now people will read my field reports. That's what my ego hopes. But it's more than just ego gratification. It's a means of communication and finding out if other guys are seeing this girl. If he reads what I did, then maybe he'll share something with me."

The Internet had spawned an unprecedented opportunity for prostitutes' clients to consort with one another. The pursuit of sex for sale has been, historically, a very private and furtive activity for men, from the lone motorist cruising Los Angeles's Sunset Boulevard surveying curbside street prostitutes to the stealthy attorney ducking into an escort agency on his lunch hour. Johns have kept to themselves, in large part because of social stigma. But now, Bashful's website offered both experienced and new customers a safe, anonymous way to fraternize, to confess their secret liaisons, and to share their reflections and concerns. Electronic communication gave johns an opportunity for camaraderie and peer acceptance, free from shame.

In 1996, a man with the user name "Georgia Powers"

proposed that he and Bashful join forces to create a new web-site, the Georgia Powers Bordello Connection (http://www. gppays.com). In addition to having links to Bashful's original FAQ, his library of field reports, and regularly updated work schedules for specific brothel prostitutes, their new site hosted an interactive bulletin board, the Georgia Powers Message Board. Initially only a couple of messages were posted per week, but traffic eventually picked up to over two hundred messages posted daily. "Flyfisher," "Interested Bystander," "Big Bamboo," and "Asbestos Moth" were among about seventy-eight active online posters, while the number of lurkers, those who only read the site, is unknown. Until now, access to the candid, unguarded thought processes of johns has been a privilege afforded only to psychotherapists.

I was surprised to learn that a handful of brothel prostitutes had also begun posting regularly on the message board. For women to engage in cyber-chat with customers defied the oldest principle of the profession, maintaining separate professional and personal worlds. Not surprisingly, women initially chose to communicate online with customers as a business tool. Annabella, the first brothel prostitute to join the Cyber-WhoreMongers online in June 1996, said it had been her initial intention to cultivate business contacts through this new medium and to begin setting up online parties with brothel customers by appointment. In time, Annabella became a deity to the CyberWhoreMongers; she was the brothel prostitute with the most field reports—forty-seven in all. At the start, she had been careful not to engage in extended message board dialogue with clients, although they were all too eager to interrogate her about both her personal life and her high prices.

But to chat freely was exactly what the next two prostitutes who came online had in mind. Almost a year after Annabella first logged on, Daisy and Fernanda posted to the message board, an event that ultimately changed both the volume and the tone of the message board communications. According to Bashful, "That's when the message board exploded from twenty messages a day to two hundred. Suddenly, men's interest skyrocketed. The 'Girls Aren't Allowed' sign had come down! Because neither one was still working in the brothels, they were completely free to say whatever they wanted. Daisy blasted the Mustang Ranch every which way but loose. Fernanda did to varying degrees as well. And we simply loved it. Where else in cyberspace or anywhere else in the world, can people, even ordinary squares, come along and actually talk to real live prostitutes? And without having to pay them? So people were really excited about it."

I remembered Daisy. She had been one of Baby's nightshift colleagues, the one who'd handed out tongue-in-cheek "whore" awards. We'd met on my first trip. A petite, energetic brunette with cropped, boyish hair, she had challenged me to defend the rationale of my condom research. We were alone together in the parlor, where I was describing the study in an attempt to convince her to participate. In the middle of my pitch, she interrupted. "Who cares about condoms? I don't know why you're doing this study. You should be doing a psychological study about why we got into prostitution in the first place." I hadn't known what to say. Daisy volunteered her own analysis: most of her peers were either adopted or military brats. She then offered the oft-asserted correlation between prostitution and a history of sexual abuse in childhood; she professed that it applied to brothel workers as well. She finished with a fierce diatribe against the brothels for their role in perpetuating the business of prostitution and in pimping women. Not surprisingly, Daisy refused to participate in my condom study, and I never saw her again at Mustang after that trip.

Now, Daisy and Fernanda were using the message board to stir things up. The two women said they were out to set the record straight, to correct the CyberWhoreMongers' misconceptions about prostitution, sex, men, and women. According to Fernanda, "Coincidentally, Daisy and I ended up online at the same time. We were the first women who really spent any amount of time there. All these old-fogy fuckers sitting around bullshitting about LPIN [licensed prostitution in Nevada] had no idea what was really going on. They were just reiterating all these stereotypes and bullshit."

A twenty-seven-year-old tomboy with short, wildly curly, honey-blond hair, Fernanda had a mischievous grin that only hinted at her chutzpah. After being kicked out of her adoptive parents' home at fourteen, she had hitchhiked from New England to Florida, and ultimately found herself smuggling alcohol and tobacco out of the United States with her boyfriend, who later became her husband. He was caught; Fernanda fled to Nevada to escape prosecution and became a prostitute at Mustang Ranch to cover her husband's mounting legal expenses. One of the most outspoken women at Mustang, Fernanda regularly challenged brothel management's authority. During her first two weeks of work, she broke a customer's nose when he bit her nipple. After she had earned enough money to cover her husband's bills, Fernanda formally left him, prompted by his fury that she had resorted to prostitution. In the meantime, she had found a new family in her Mustang colleagues.

Of the online postings, Fernanda said: "[Daisy and I] came in and were like, 'Oh no, fuck that. You guys have got it all wrong. The houses don't give a shit about us, are you kidding? You've got your blinders on.' So, we started telling them what was really going down."

The Internet offered brothel prostitutes like Fernanda long-awaited autonomy to promote and broker their business. And, shielded from retaliation by management, Fernanda and Daisy and later others could express their opinions freely and air their grievances about self-serving brothel owners and poor work conditions. The women sought to squelch unfair and dangerous misinformation, such as claims of rampant, concealed sexually transmitted diseases among brothel prostitutes.

More interestingly to me, they let loose their feelings about the profession, and their clients—feelings I had heard few other brothel prostitutes express, especially *to* their customers. When a man posted a message asking how she really felt about being a prostitute, Daisy replied: "The first words that come to mind are: degraded, dehumanized, used, victim, ashamed, humiliated, embarrassed, insulted, slave, rape, violated. I know these words are hard to you . . . but I just closed my eyes and

typed the words that come into my mind." She went on to describe her true thoughts about brothel customers: "99% of
them fit these words: pig, dog, animal, uncaring, user, slave
owner, asshole, mean, thoughtless, rude, crude, blind."

Stunned by Daisy's frank communication, CyberWhore-
Mongers flooded the message board with humble, apologetic
replies. Typical was that of a man with the user name GS: "It
makes me take a good hard look at myself, and I don't like
what I see. It is posts like this one, and your previous posts
about your feelings that open our eyes. I hate that I have contributed to making a woman feel this way."

As more prostitutes posted to the board, they united in
teaching the men brothel customer etiquette and admonished
any man who used the message board to exhibit disrespect for
prostitutes. One man with the handle XL wrote: "I was
shocked and offended when Fernanda and Daisy first came on
the board. They were hitting us over the head with some of the
behind-the-scenes reality of licensed prostitution in Nevada
(LPIN), which some of us preferred to ignore and others never
knew existed. It needed to be offensive to get the point
across—the medium of crudeness and anger was as much the
message as the facts were. Eventually I got it. They completely
changed the tenor and personality of the board and have influ-
enced our view and knowledge of LPIN as much as anyone."

Where once the all-male cyber-community was almost
unconditionally accepting of one another, now the men began
turning on one another in shows of gallantry. The message
board grew cluttered with posts from men blasting each other's

ideas and reprimanding one another for being insensitive. Bashful even submitted to the prostitutes' requests and removed all mention of prices from the field reports. By publicly disclosing prices on the Internet, Bashful had intended to expose the brothels' pricing system as a shell game that kept consumers guessing as to real prices, and to enable novice brothel visitors to make more informed choices. Now, his critics contended, he had forsaken his original mission in order to "kiss the girls' asses" so as not to have "a bunch of girls mad at him." Much antagonistic discussion on the message board followed before Bashful decided to try to strike a balance between the interests of the clients and those of brothel workers. He posted the general results of a pricing survey he had conducted among the CyberWhoreMongers, which revealed that men's parties cost an average of $335 an hour and 90 percent of them ranged between $150 and $500 an hour.

Despite all their bickering, the CyberWhoreMongers and a handful of prostitutes had become a tight-knit virtual community. "In the long haul," Bashful posted on the message board, "we seem to have become a family that fights a lot but still has a remarkably warm and cohesive quality to it. My best friends are members of our community." Because of the illicit and confessional nature of their conversations, the CyberWhore-Mongers found themselves bound by a sense of intimacy and vulnerability. In addition to their usual titillating discussions and playful banter, individuals began to use the message board to ask for support during serious life crises, ranging from romantic breakups to health problems. One man who went by the handle Clatch claimed his cyber friends offered more moral support after his heart attack than did people in his everyday life. "After I got home from the hospital, I checked the message board and I was astounded to see so much concern about me. People asking each other where I was, saying things like 'This isn't like him to go this long without posting.' In some senses, I have gotten to know these people better than people in my real life."

But in spite of their burgeoning sense of kinship, the community was still only a virtual one, until one day in 1997 when Bashful proposed a real-life meeting, a rendezvous in Nevada to go brothel-hopping together. Only twelve men showed up that first year; many others were too apprehensive about both losing their anonymity and doing the unimaginable—going to a brothel to consort with other men. But the twelve who took the dare found immense satisfaction in chatting about computers and swapping stories about their favorite brothel prostitutes before heading out together en masse to the Ranches and partying with each other's recommendations, including Annabella and Fernanda. "My days of solitary brothel cruising came to an end," one man posted afterward, "and I learned the joy of hanging out in whorehouses with the guys." Thus was born the annual CyberWhoreMongers Convention.

The second annual convention promised to be different. Bashful expected many more men—regular posters as well as lurkers—to make an appearance. Rather than simply congregating at a different brothel each night, the CyberWhoreMongers filled their four-day fête with scheduled events, from an awards dinner on Friday night to a Saturday afternoon barbecue. Perhaps most extraordinary, however, was the fact that some of the men's favorite working girls planned to attend the convention as participants.

I was deeply curious to see who CyberWhoreMongers were. Sure enough, many of the men I met at the convention were computer programmers and software designers, but there were also lawyers, pharmacists, and truck drivers. To my shock, I even met a man from my own stomping ground: a Harvard Medical School alumnus and faculty member named Daniel. Naturally concerned about his reputation, Daniel was initially mortified to meet me. He didn't want to tell me at which Harvard hospital he attended. Should I ever choose to "out" him back in Boston, he said, I would ruin his career. Eventually, however, he relaxed, and he ended up talking my ear off for over five hours, a soliloquy that was half philosophical self-reflection, half shamed confessional.

Daniel first discovered brothel prostitution when he stumbled across the Georgia Powers website two years earlier, on the heels of a painful divorce. "I was just so depressed. I had sacrificed so much to attain professional success, and then I felt I sacrificed my profession in attempts to have a happy marriage—futilely." Brothel prostitution helped restore his sense of manhood and self-confidence, he said, while the CyberWhoreMongers provided him with a sense of camaraderie that relieved some of his shame. Believing he was probably the only Harvard physician who patronized Nevada's brothels, Daniel suspected his colleagues would have been even more appalled to learn he had actually fallen for Fernanda. Only recently had Daniel come to terms with the fact

226 •• ALEXA ALBERT

that they would never become lovers. Still, he continued to care deeply for her. "I can't recall a friend who has made me feel so completely accepted and comfortable to be around as Fernanda."

The mood was jovial throughout the course of the entire convention. Insider jokes abounded, such as the lapel pins in the shape of miniature carrots handed out to everyone, an allusion to a story Daisy once posted about a client who wanted anal sex with a carrot; she screwed him so hard he bled. Even lurkers came forth. One, who called himself John (he had no user name, since he had never posted), bought so many raffle tickets—fifteen—that he won the prize, a free outdate with Baby's friend Savannah. As the convention came to a close and people began departing, handshakes and back pats turned into bear hugs and kisses.

As I drove back to Mustang after the weekend ended, I questioned my decision to attend the convention. While I enjoyed the company immensely, I wondered if I'd been duped. What did women like Tanya and Linda always say—"A trick is always a trick"? Many of the prostitutes at Mustang disliked the field reports, believing that the reviews worked to their disadvantage no matter what. A marginal review could cost them potential clients, while a good report could build unrealistic expectations that led to dissatisfaction and disgruntlement. Despite numerous glowing reports of her work, even Baby had had a few men come in and say disappointedly, "You're much older than Bashful made you sound." During the convention, the men angered a number of prostitutes at Mustang Ranch when they acted more interested in hanging out in the parlor talking among themselves than in partying with the women. " 'So *you're* Uncle Bob,' " said one woman, mocking an exchange she'd heard the night before. " 'You're my hero. I love you.' "

Mustang management cursed the men for an entirely different reason. Bashful and friends had assumed that brothel owners would appreciate the free publicity furnished by their website. Instead, owners worried that the information could actually endanger the brothel industry. Posting specific prostitutes' work schedules could be interpreted as a form of advertisement, which was illegal. According to George Flint, the men's frank discussion about controversial aspects of the business posed another potential liability for the industry. For example, the men's heated discussions of whether or not "bareback" blow jobs and intercourse ever occurred could be used as evidence against the brothels by opponents like John Reese or Senator O'Donnell.

And how beneficial was this association for the men, really? It certainly ate up their time. Bashful figured he spent at least five hours a day on the message board, two hours at work and three hours at home. For all that this cyber community offered its members, I suspected it actually hampered further social development. Men felt justified in devoting inordinate amounts of time to being online with others equally obsessed with brothel prostitution. Bashful, for example, had only had sex with prostitutes, a fact he almost sounded proud of when he told his cyber friends. Daisy once posted a very frank, unflattering picture of the CyberWhoreMongers: "I think that about 80% of the men on this board have given up and are taking the easy way out. This group of guys has replaced a normal, healthy social life with licensed prostitution in Nevada. I feel bad for them. You don't have to pay for 'love' and attention. Sure there are a lot of you out there that are not Brad Pitt . . . but you are people. Overweight? Balding? Socially shy? Get over it, go meet someone that will love you for real. You deserve it, we all do."

The Internet was also straining the old boundaries of the prostitute-client relationship in ways that could be frightening. Annabella learned this firsthand soon after the convention, when she received a threat from a former CyberWhoreMonger who had the user name Chisel. A wealthy married man, Chisel had frequently contributed field reports about Annabella, his favorite brothel prostitute, to Bashful's original website. As his obsession with her grew, Chisel cut ties with the CyberWhore-Mongers to start another website devoted to prostitution. Soon afterward, he began demanding that Annabella quit prostitution and become his mistress. When she refused, and subsequently refused to further service him, Chisel decided if he couldn't have Annabella no one else would. (Most of the other men who posted lacked possessiveness. As Bashful put it, "If you are territorial or possessive you aren't going to like this medium; you aren't going to want to tell other guys about the great girls.") Chisel threatened to post Annabella's real name and other personal information he had secured unless she agreed to stop posting on the CyberWhoreMongers' message board and to have all her field reports deleted.

Despite pleas—thirty-six posts in all—from other men to leave her alone, Chisel wouldn't let up, and Annabella finally gave in. In a final post on the Georgia Powers message board, she wrote: "At one time, I thought him [Chisel] to be a friend, as close as any of you I have held dear. I trusted him and shared much of my life with him. As time went on he proved that he had another agenda. . . . His terrorism has become too much for me. . . . I have requested that all my reports be pulled, I will no longer post to this message board and I have given notice to Marvin [owner of the Sagebrush brothel] that I have retired as of today. This was a heartbreaking decision. I was looking forward to at least one or two more years in the business. I have met some wonderful people, some very very dear people. I will never forget any of you. I need to make a complete break though. No one can imagine the stress I have been put through. I must put all of this behind me. . . . It is with tears that I bid all of you farewell."

The circumstances of Annabella's retirement were indeed rare. But calling it quits and giving up the business was unusual for brothel prostitutes regardless of the circumstances. In fact, during my six years of involvement, I saw very few members of the brothel community leave Mustang Ranch. They were all too hooked.

10 .. HOOKED

In the spring of 1999, Mustang Ranch went on trial. For almost a decade, the federal government had suspected that Joe Conforte had covertly repurchased his brothel at the IRS's 1990 auction with $1.49 million he had smuggled abroad. But the U.S. attorney had no proof until recently, when new evidence surfaced that Conforte was still controlling and profiting from Mustang Ranch despite his fugitive status in South America. Specifically, Conforte's former attorney and bookkeeper, both of whom had been facing federal indictments, copped pleas and testified that Conforte had siphoned off over $4 million from Mustang Ranch between 1993 and 1996 through checks and wire transfers sent by brothel employees to his associates in South America.

I was at home in Boston when I received a phone call from George Flint letting me know the trial was over and the verdict decided. In less than ten hours, the federal jury had found the current Mustang owners (A.G.E. Enterprises, Inc., and its holding company, A.G.E. Corp., Inc.) guilty of racketeering crimes that included international money laundering, bankruptcy fraud, and domestic as well as foreign wire fraud with Joe Conforte as beneficiary.* The A.G.E. companies were merely shell corporations, federal prosecutors had successfully argued, set up in order to hide Conforte's true proprietorship. And the upshot of all this, George explained, was that in less than thirty days, the federal government planned to seize the brothel and lock its doors for good.

News of Conforte's active involvement with Mustang Ranch didn't surprise me. Ever since my first visit, I had gathered that Conforte played a role in day-to-day operations. Despite his physical absence, his presence was ubiquitous, from the daunting black-and-white portrait with trademark cigar in hand that hung prominently in the parlor to the almost daily check-in calls that George and others fielded.†

Still, I hadn't expected the trial to turn out like this. Almost no one had. George had told me about the federal gov-

---

*The ownership had undergone several name changes after Victor Perry acquired the brothel from the IRS in 1990.

†Conforte explained that his close involvement with Mustang Ranch was his legal right as a paid "consultant" to the shareholders of the operating company, A.G.E. This succeeded in keeping the federal government at bay until 1998, a period of almost ten years.

ernment's preoccupation with nabbing Conforte, but given Conforte's extraordinary survival record, no one could quite believe he would ever go down. Hadn't Louis, the brothel's cook, told me, "Mustang's like a cat with nine lives. No matter what happens, it always rises from the ashes." Only George voiced doubts. "Whorehouses never win in court," he said unequivocally. As I listened to George dolefully explain the case, the people whose lives would be affected by the closing flashed through my mind. Where would everyone go? What would they do?

What did locals think about the demise of one of their state's most noted institutions and landmarks? According to George, public reaction to the impending closure of Mustang Ranch was mixed. Long contemptuous of Conforte, the *Reno Gazette-Journal* wrote in a scathing editorial:

> The only way we can be assured that the last chapter has been written in the long, sorry saga of the Mustang Ranch is for the federal government to tear it down. . . . Only when the Mustang is gone will we know that Joe Conforte's ugly influence over Storey County will have been ended once and for all. The federal government . . . will be doing northern Nevada a huge favor by calling in the wrecking crew. As the Mustang is demolished, Storey County leaders can look clear-eyed at the real cost of their decades-long dance with Conforte.

Others in the community less fixated on Conforte also viewed Mustang's closure as a moral victory. "I would like to see this historic day as the beginning of the end of the brothels in Nevada," announced a woman named Barbara Jones, a member of Reno's Sunrise Fellowship and Point of Grace Church, at the Storey County commissioners' meeting. She went on to assure the commissioners that God would handle any resultant financial setback. "If we take the right stand, the blessings will come. I believe it will be taken care of. It's not very specific for people who like specifics, but sometimes God doesn't work that way."

Not all locals agreed. A poll conducted by the *Gazette-Journal* of over two thousand readers found that only 28 percent thought Mustang Ranch should be shut down, while 71 percent opposed the closure. Some defended Mustang as a relic of Nevada's past that should be preserved. Others worried about the financial repercussions to Storey County. To make up for the lost revenue from fees for brothel and liquor licenses and work cards, said the Storey County Commission chairman, Chuck Haynes, the county might need to increase property taxes, reduce sheriff or fire department budgets, close the auditor's office, or stop paying the street lighting bill. Reno shopkeepers and law enforcement grumbled about a likely mushrooming of street prostitution when Mustang working girls had nowhere else to go.

The ruling judge in the case, U.S. District Judge Howard McKibben, delayed the forfeiture for thirty days to give employees time to relocate. Unfortunately, the delay only gave members of the brothel false hope. Behind Mustang's eight-foot wrought-iron fences, women and staff were insulated from the local scuttlebutt save for what they saw on the nightly news, read in the newspaper, or heard from their clients. Did defense attorneys really have new "explosive" evidence that could prompt the judge to reverse the verdict? Was it true that during deliberations, one of the jurors had been pushed up against a wall by another and told, "If you don't vote to convict, God's going to get you"? The brothel's mood oscillated between despair and optimism.

George had already received more than three dozen phone calls from people interested in buying Mustang Ranch, but the government's final plans for the brothel were as yet undetermined. For now, it would keep up the seized property until the court issued a final order of forfeiture, which in turn would follow consideration of all monetary claims against the property and appeals by defendants. It was rumored that Conforte had already put the squeeze on his nephew David Burgess, owner of the Old Bridge Ranch, to hand over his brothel or else Conforte would force the county commissioners to outlaw prostitution in Storey County altogether. True to his egotistical character, Conforte allegedly felt entitled to reclaim what once was his—or at least, what he thought he deserved to have as the father of legalized prostitution in Storey County.

Brothel opponents like John Reese hoped the county might use this opportunity to outlaw brothels altogether, though none of the three commissioners had shown much enthusiasm for that. But George was worried. "The legislature's support is not necessarily support of the industry as much as it's support of the mystique of Mustang Ranch," he explained to me on the phone. "In other words, I don't think the legislators give a hoot or a holler about Billie's Day and Night." (Billie's was a hole-in-the-wall brothel in southern Nevada with no more than three prostitutes at a time, run by a toothless seventy-eight-year-old madam named Opal Radcliffe.) Because Mustang subsidized most of his lobbying budget, George anticipated feeling crippled, depleted of ammunition to defend the industry from its opponents. "How the heck am I going to support this industry if I don't have any bullets in my gun?"

I hadn't visited Mustang for almost a year, and I took the next plane to Reno for what I assumed would be a final good-bye. No one seemed surprised when I rang the doorbell twice and appeared suddenly in Mustang #1's parlor. The women and staff greeted me with hugs and warm smiles. I was pleased and surprised to see many familiar faces; George had mentioned over the telephone that a handful of women left immediately after the verdict, not wanting to remain in limbo for another thirty days. But practically everyone I knew was still there: Baby, Brittany, Tanya, Linda, Donna, Eva, and Mercedes.

George believed some of the women "sincerely and naïvely thought God was going to split the seas, that Moses was going to walk across dry land, and that there was going to be a miracle." When I asked a prostitute named Josie where she planned to relocate, she chastised me for bringing such "negative energy" into the brothel. Mustang was going to survive, she said;

we just needed to believe and have faith. I wanted to believe her, but I hesitated to put too much trust in her spiritual insights. On a previous visit, Josie had told me about the prophetic voices that spoke to her and divulged that Hillary Clinton would soon come out as a lesbian, while Bill would be president for a *third* term.

Most of the working girls still at Mustang felt a strong sense of obligation to the brothel. "I want to make sure the ship's down before I desert it," said Linda. Even the normally tough Tanya showed her emotions. "It's sad leaving people that I know so well," she said. "It's like one big home or family. My body, her body, and a lot of other girls' bodies built this business back up over the last nine years to what it is. Now it's like it's being kicked apart again."

Even relative newcomers like Eva, the woman I'd accompanied when she got licensed several years earlier, expressed similar feelings. "I'm sad because these are all my sisters," she said, weepy and red-eyed. "I'm definitely depressed. I've never had sisterhood like this. They love you no matter what you do—it's unconditional love. Sure, we all fight. We get into our little tiffs and irritate each other, but that's how sisters are. Now I'm losing my sisters and I feel like I'm moving away from home."

While everyone worried about losing their jobs, genuine concern for one another prevailed. No one knew who had it worse. Tanya told me she felt more for the employees who had worked at Mustang for years. What sort of conventional work was someone like Blanche, in her mid-fifties with almost two decades of floor maid experience, qualified for? It was unlikely that Nevada's remaining brothels could absorb Mustang's seventy-five staff members. Most of the employees had families in nearby Reno and Sparks and had no desire to relocate. Even jobs with transferrable skills, like bartending, explained Brian, would be hard to get with Mustang—a "whorehouse" to the outside world—on your résumé.

Remarkably, in spite of everyone's anxiety, I was hard-pressed to find much hostility directed at Joe Conforte. Most women were more incensed that the IRS had wasted taxpayers' money all these years hunting down a seventy-three-year-old man. To an outsider, though, it seemed all too obvious that Conforte hadn't shown the same loyalty. His criminal activities over the years had hurt innocent people, and by refusing to come home, he had sacrificed others, including a longtime associate, sixty-two-year-old Shirley Colletti. A former Mustang manager and Storey County commissioner, Colletti had been convicted along with the A.G.E. companies of conspiring to conceal Conforte's ownership of Mustang and illegally transferring millions of dollars to him. Judge McKibben ordered Colletti to forfeit $220,000 in cash and sentenced her to almost four years in federal prison. Had Conforte turned himself in, it's unlikely the government would have bothered picking on underlings like her.

Even now Conforte persisted in baiting the government; he insisted that George place an advertisement for him in the *Reno Gazette-Journal* that read, "A man can be destroyed but he will not be defeated. Joe Conforte."

Business hadn't been the same since the verdict. The doorbell rang frequently, but most of the men gravitated to the bar and seemed content to gape. But if sex wasn't selling, Mustang souvenirs were. Men bought T-shirts, key chains, shot glasses, bumper stickers, and postcards by the handful.

But the women were too distracted to care. They sat huddled together around the parlor whispering about their career options and making telephone calls to other brothels to set up interviews. Most Mustang prostitutes wanted to remain in northern Nevada, so they deliberated between moving to neighboring Old Bridge Ranch or to one of Lyon County's four brothels.

In the first weeks after the verdict, many of the women acted out, blowing off house rules, ignoring calls to line up, giving the floor maids grief, and openly using drugs. Money-stashing was rampant, as women rationalized they were only stealing from the government. "What are they going to do, fire me?" women asked.

By the last week, however, the frenzy had given way to somber resignation. Louis, the women's favorite cook, who was not scheduled to work, had opted to come in anyway. All the vendors came by to pay their final respects, among them Ann Marie, Mustang's Avon representative for over twenty-six years, who earned her living selling lipsticks, fragrances, and bubble bath exclusively to Mustang prostitutes.

Leo showed up and began unloading his usual store of bodysuits, slip dresses, and lingerie as if it were any other Saturday. I couldn't imagine who he thought would be interested at a time like this, but he was philosophical: "You think they're going to go home and sit and cry since this place is closing? By Monday or Tuesday, they'll be working someplace else." Meanwhile, Leo had his own troubles. A.G.E. companies had been ordered to forfeit not only Mustang Ranch and $40 million cash, but also all A.G.E.-owned real estate. Lockwood Mobile Home Park residents like Leo, many of whom were fixed-income retirees, risked losing their now $90-a-month homes.

Like Leo, the women shifted into work mode for the final weekend. Anticipating that men would flock to the brothel for one last hurrah, the women put on their nicest outfits. As they'd expected, the doorbell rang constantly from seven P.M. on, and the bar filled with paying customers. Men pulled out wads of bills, splurging one last time. For the first time all week, I saw genuine smiles come over the women's faces. The parlor hummed as women crisscrossed the deep red carpet, leading men to their bedrooms and returning alone to deposit money with the cashier. By eleven P.M., the bar was so busy that the floor maid decided to forgo lineups altogether. At one point, about a hundred men were standing shoulder to shoulder in the bar waiting for prostitutes to free up.

Most of these men were Mustang regulars, like Ernie, an eighty-year-old known for his tendency to overdrink and then conk out on a parlor sofa. He came in Saturday night wearing a flamingo pink T-shirt that read I ♥ HOOKERS—a gift he'd received from Lara, his favorite Mustang prostitute. As usual, he told a few crude jokes, then toppled over on a couch, where he slept for over an hour. When he awoke, Lara smoothly and tenderly guided him back to her room. I wondered where this old man would turn for sex and companionship now.

When Stewart and Roger sauntered in, promptly at eight,

they stood stupefied at the sight of so many other men. They had spent the previous weeks trying to get used to neighboring Old Bridge Ranch, but they assumed that as faithful regulars they would have their pickings of Mustang prostitutes for one last go-round. Both had hopes of using up their remaining Mustang passes. Even several CyberWhoreMongers showed up.

Not all visitors were greeted enthusiastically on this final Saturday night. The rival brothel owner Dennis Hof paraded into Mustang to gloat over the demise of his competition. The floor maid on duty scowled when she saw him stroll through the door accompanied by an entourage of men, including Ron Jeremy, a porn star who was involved in Hof's X-rated film business. "I don't think they should have been allowed in here," the floor maid later told me. "I felt like I was a dying horse and they were the vultures swarming over me."

Hof had come to savor his triumph. "With Mustang Ranch closing, we're the heir apparent," Dennis had boasted to reporters. "We're going to take over where Mustang left off, except in a classy manner." He went on to say that his manager had already interviewed forty-five Mustang prostitutes but in the end only hired five. "Only the best," he said. "We're going to be classier than the Mustang ever was." All that night, he sidled up to prostitutes to introduce himself and offer his electric pink business card. His agenda was excruciatingly obvious—for all his talk of selectivity, he was here to scout the girls.

Although business boomed into the wee hours of the

morning, by noon Sunday all thought was on clearing out. Despite some talk about sticking it out to the bitter end and forming a human chain around the brothel to fend off the IRS, most women had decided to leave before the media animals descended. Ryder trucks and U-Hauls pulled into the parking lot, where women worked together to load their belongings—television sets, comforters, lamps, and garbage bags stuffed with clothes. Baby managed to persuade Philip, her devoted regular, to orchestrate her move. He pulled up in a U-Haul early in the morning and spent all day moving Baby's possessions with tremendous delicacy into the truck. Meanwhile—she was among a handful of women still working—Baby used the bedroom next door to hers to party with customers. Philip lurked outside the door, trying to eavesdrop, every time he came to retrieve a new load.

As if it were the morning of the last day of summer camp, women dashed around exchanging addresses and snapping photos with their disposable cameras. Some women hugged and kissed good-bye; others slipped out quietly.

By late afternoon, most of the women had left. Twenty-one remained, only three or four of whom were actually working the floor, while the rest either packed or slept. The cook at Mustang #2 had left without warning, so the working girls there had no warm dinner. By evening, management decided to shut down the annex and send the girls over to #1. As Louis closed down the kitchen at #1 for the night, I heard him muttering to himself how empty he felt inside, "like a part of me is going away." Mustang felt dead.

At around ten on Monday morning, August 9, 1999, three federal agents appeared to pick up the last bank deposit from the weekend. Since the verdict, the U.S. Customs Agency had been handling Mustang's books, counting all the money and signing all the checks. Although the brothel wasn't to be handed over until 5:01 P.M., Bob Del Carlo, A.G.E.'s new president, who had been the Storey County sheriff for twenty-eight years, decided to close it down after the pickup. The rest of the afternoon was to be devoted to housecleaning. This made sense to brothel management, since the money would be going straight into the hands of the U.S. government anyway, and there were only a few women still interested in turning tricks. Money from Mustang's last official customer was booked at 10:20 A.M.

Early in the morning, crowds had begun to form outside Mustang #1's gate. Tourists and locals flocked for one last look. Men and women got out of their cars to pose for photographs in front of the brothel. These gawking sightseers camping outside the brothel gates hoping to snap a photo of one of America's curiosities, a licensed prostitute, reminded me again of how disconnected these women were from the rest of society. The pink souvenir trailer stationed in the parking lot had sold out of Mustang merchandise, save for one extra-extra-large white golf T-shirt with the Mustang logo over the breast pocket.

Media trucks with satellite dishes from NBC, ABC, and Fox affiliates sat parked in front of the brothel. Reporters stood outside the front gates, desperate for sound bites from anyone who passed through. Customers who'd thought the brothel would be open for business until five P.M. were turned away disappointed after learning they couldn't even get a drink at the bar. Many tried to shield their faces from the cameras. In an act of defiance, Baby managed to sneak one latecomer into her room to turn a final trick several hours after the Feds had closed out Mustang's register. She smiled triumphantly at me ninety minutes later as she walked Mustang's last, unofficial customer back to the front gate.

By noon, when George arrived, most of the women had cleared out. He invited the media inside the front gate for a press conference. He spoke about "the sadness of the day" and "the breakup of a family." A few women chose to participate in the interviews, including Baby. Her mother had died recently and she had no one else she needed to protect from the truth of her profession.

Not long before five, I wandered back through Mustang one last time while the staff gathered together in the kitchen. The hallways were still and the bedroom doors flung open. Inside, beds were stripped down to the mattresses, save for some rooms where pillows and blankets had been abandoned. Discarded clothing and business cards were scattered on the floor. The brothel had been deserted.

At precisely five, Bob Del Carlo announced it was time for us all to leave. "Let's walk out together one last time," he said. Single file, we emerged from the brothel and faced a swelling crowd of sixty or so. I'm not quite sure how I ended up marching out with the remaining seventeen brothel workers, but I did. After we all passed through, George shut the Mustang gate for the last time in the business's history.

Moments later, a caravan of unmarked cars full of federal agents screeched into the Mustang parking lots. IRS, FBI, and U.S. Customs officials poured out, their bulletproof vests bulging beneath their suits. Three agents stayed outside to guard the gates; the rest rushed inside. About twenty minutes later, James Collie, chief of the Criminal Investigation Division for the Southwest District IRS, emerged from the brothel, issued a press release, and briefly answered reporters' questions. Five minutes later, he hopped into his sedan and sped away. It was final.

THAT NIGHT I watched the evening news in a Reno motel room as I repacked my belongings in preparation for an early flight home the next day. A short clip showed the brothel's padlocked gates. The news anchor capped the closure with a shrug and a jab: "It's just a bunch of hookers, all they have to do is find another corner to make a living on."

I wanted to scream. *Don't you realize that by eliminating Mustang Ranch, you don't simply displace "a bunch of hookers"? You eradicate a community, a family!*

The brothel had provided an income as well as friendship, compassion, trust, and hope for countless women and men. In many ways, Mustang Ranch picked up where society had dropped the ball. It had provided a safe, nonjudgmental, economically sound work environment and a fair way for a community of several dozen women and their families to meet their most basic needs.

Legal brothels are one alternative in dealing with prostitution. However disturbing the idea of commercial sex may be to some of us, it's naïve to believe that prostitution can ever be eliminated. The demand will be met with supply one way or another, no matter what is legislated. Turning our backs on the women (and men) who do this work may be far more immoral—even criminal—than prostitution itself. Only when we recognize and validate the work of professional prostitutes can we expect them to practice their trade safely and responsibly.

My time at Mustang Ranch proved to me just how complicated human sexuality and everything about it can be, especially how it eludes total understanding. Consensual sex between adults—whether for pay or pro bono—is exactly that, consensual. As such, it's a personal and private decision. What seems universally to be true about it is our need to supercharge it politically and load it down with the heavy freight of moral issues.

Baby once told me that she wanted to make it known that she and her colleagues were "okay people, too." Perhaps her point was best made in a phone call we shared not long after Mustang's closing. "I feel like I've made a difference in my clients' lives. That they can breathe easier each night. I appreciate these guys and I feel they don't see me as a hooker or prostitute, but see me as a person, as Baby. That makes me feel worthy—not only as a prostitute or working girl but as a human being."

This was my experience also: seeing the women of Mustang Ranch as human beings. In a business built largely on desire and fantasy, it's easy to be deceived by our assumptions and, in doing so, overlook the humanity that's at the core of this complex and timeless profession.

EPILOGUE

Nearly three years after its closure, Mustang Ranch sits vacant and silent. In July 2001, the Ninth U.S. Circuit Court of Appeals in San Francisco ruled in favor of upholding money-laundering and racketeering convictions against brothel parent companies A.G.E. Enterprises, Inc. and A.G.E. Corp., Inc., and former Mustang manager Shirley Colletti. Until the U.S. Supreme Court decides whether or not to review the case, the federal government must maintain Mustang's facilities so that the brothel can reopen for business should the Court overturn the guilty verdicts. In the meantime, Colletti began serving her forty-six-month term in a minimum-security federal prison in Dublin, California, in February 2002, after the U.S. Supreme Court rejected her petition to remain free on appeal until their decision.

Ironically, Joe Conforte, the focus of the investigation that brought Mustang Ranch to its knees, appears to have gotten off scot-free. Two months after Mustang's closure, the Brazilian Supreme Court decided in an 8–0 ruling that Conforte couldn't be extradited, given the narrow terms of the extradition treaty between the United States and Brazil, which doesn't cover bankruptcy fraud. Assistant U.S. Attorney Greg Damm, one of the case's chief prosecutors, more or less admits defeat and concedes the federal government may never get their day in court with Conforte. Meanwhile, Conforte continues to grumble from abroad that if he can't run a brothel in Storey County, no one else should either.

Despite Conforte's grousing, Storey County commissioners recently decided to issue a new brothel license. With the loss of once-sizable revenue after Mustang's closure, the county initially coped financially by imposing a wage and hiring freeze in order to stay within its annual budget. However, Storey County now hopes to generate $300,000 in annual tax revenues from the proposed new brothel, Wild Horse Canyon Ranch & Spa, to be built on a site almost four miles from the closed Mustang Ranch. This will be the first test of Storey County's revised brothel ordinance that now requires a detailed investigation of all brothel owner applicants and the prohibition of convicted felons like Conforte from owning a brothel. The ordinance also demands any corporation that owns a brothel to reveal the names of its shareholders as well as the names of those in associated corporations.

Although the new owner's license application passed the

close scrutiny of county officials, other legal problems may doom prospects for Wild Horse Canyon Ranch & Spa. A public relations debacle ensued early on over original plans to name the new brothel after the legendary American Indian chieftain Crazy Horse. More recently, two national companies, Kal Kan Foods Inc. and Roybridge Investments, each with facilities approximately one mile away from the proposed site for the new brothel in the 102,000-acre Tahoe-Reno Industrial Park—considered the largest industrial park in North America—filed a federal lawsuit asking that the brothel license be voided. Their contention: that the brothel will hurt business, threaten the safety of employees of the park, and lower property values.

Most troublesome to George Flint isn't the fate of Storey County's newest brothel, but rather the liability it now poses to Nevada's entire brothel industry. George fears that all the media attention spawned by this incident coupled with the high-power lobbyists retained by Tahoe-Reno Industrial Park interests may be enough to pressure legislators in 2003 to consider bills that further restrict, or even outlaw, brothel prostitution. Of not much help is the recent proliferation of negative brothel press brought on in part by several of Nevada's twenty-seven currently operating brothels themselves. For example, the Sagebrush, Nevada's second-largest brothel, outside Carson City, first hit local headlines when it nearly burned to the ground after an untended candle set the complex ablaze. More recently, heavy radio and newspaper advertising for Squeeze Play, the new topless bar/dance club adjoining the brothel, has local area residents irate.

Brothel problems sprawl well beyond the north into southern Nevada as well. After Sheri's Ranch, a brothel neighboring the Chicken Ranch in Pahrump, was sold to a thirty-year Las Vegas Metro police veteran and one-time sheriff's candidate and former car dealer, the green new owner challenged industry tradition unwittingly when he announced plans to turn the brothel into a full-scale resort with an 18-hole golf course, casino, and steakhouse. Following flaming editorials in state papers, George gave the apologetic owner a crash course in brothel survival tactics while attempting to do damage control with the press; Sheri's owner now redirects all media inquiries to George.

Despite Mack and Angel Moore's supposed righteous intentions, a sting operation busted them for selling outdates at Angel's Ladies in Nye County, where doing so is illegal. The licensing board ultimately voted to close the brothel for two weeks and fined the owners $35,000. (Angel's Ladies appeared in the press again after an appeals judge reversed the convictions of the three employees who were found guilty of prostitution-related charges off brothel premises, declaring the police sting operation entrapment.)

And then there's always Dennis Hof, of course. Hof finally shut down his XXX-movie enterprise when county officials threatened to revoke his brothel license on grounds that his license allowed only the sale of prostitution, not the filming of pornography. Still, his publicity stunts haven't stopped. His newest scheme is to get brothel prostitutes to appear on the *Howard Stern Show*, including most recently a mother-daughter team; Stern staged an on-the-air contest for a listener to win sex with both women.

Aggravated by the glare of unwanted publicity, George organized two brothel-owner meetings in the last six months to discuss "ways to preserve and improve our industry." Even though the 2001 state legislative session proved less contentious than George anticipated, with no significant anti-brothel legislation proposed, the meetings' agendas addressed George's apprehensions and emphasized the need for political savvy in order to restore the industry's public image, with formal presentations entitled "Friends, enemies and trends in the legislature" and "How to deal with the media: Low vs. high profile."

Ironically, Nevada's brothel opponents have also suffered variously since Mustang's closure. After his botched attempt to stage his own disappearance, Reese filed for bankruptcy and stopped making restitution payments to the county for the cost of his search party. One day George received a letter from Reese sent from Marathon, Florida, where he'd relocated: "It is the farthest place from Reno . . . I'm tired of getting laughed at by my friends, the press, and ostracized from every church I try to attend . . . My enemy was not the brothel association . . . It was the people I most cherished . . . The church people in Reno. When they rejected me it was like losing my closest friends on earth." Reese informed George he was working as a pizza deliveryman and sleeping in his car to save money for flying lessons.

Not long afterwards, Reese became international news

when he stole a Cessna 172 from a Florida Keys flight school and crash-landed more than one hundred miles away on a beach in Cuba. The note left behind in his car stated his intention to kidnap Fidel Castro. After U.S. diplomats negotiated for days with Cuban officials for Reese's repatriation, a U.S. District Court judge ordered him to serve six months in prison with three years probation and to pay $45,000 in damages. It later came out for the first time that Reese had a history of manic depression and periodic disappearances from home when he stopped taking his medication.

Meanwhile, back in Nevada, Senator William O'Donnell still lurks in the wings, although he's announced his intention to leave the legislature when his term ends in 2002, allegedly frustrated by his colleagues in the GOP and their ties with lobbyists.

Still, new voices of opposition continue to emerge. A grassroots movement called Citizens Against Prostitution has been formed in Nye County. Led by a youthful Pahrump pastor and several parishioners who were outraged by one owner's thinly veiled promotion of his brothel on two billboards on the outskirts of town, the group is preparing for the 2002 elections, when they plan to introduce a petition to outlaw prostitution in Nye County. They estimate that the eight thousand new transplants expected by then, with the rapid population expansion going on in and around Las Vegas, will not look kindly upon local brothels.

For the individuals associated with Mustang Ranch, it's been a mixed bag. Some have managed to quit the business. Others have found new ways to stay in the trade.

Eva is currently studying to become a hospital-based physical therapist. She told me, "I am broke most of the time, but it's cool. I don't plan on going back to the floor soon, but if I ever need to, I know it is there and I can go back."

Old-timers Tanya and Linda moved close by, to the Old Bridge Ranch, Storey County's only operating brothel, next door to Mustang. Brittany and Mercedes initially joined the Kit Kat, where they knew the acting manager, a former manager from Mustang, but both have since quit the business.

Baby relocated to another brothel outside Carson City. She quickly became one of its top bookers. Her devoted regular, Philip, continues to visit her several times a week, despite the one-hour roundtrip drive he has to make to see her.

Not all of Mustang's prostitutes are accounted for; Donna, Dinah, and Heather have simply slipped away. Because most of the women kept their real names and hometowns secret, there's no easy way to locate them.

Bashful and the other CyberWhoreMongers initially tried to keep track of Mustang prostitutes on their website, the Georgia Powers Bordello Connection. Bashful reports that the men miss the Mustang Ranch deeply. The Fifth Annual Cyber-WhoreMonger Convention in the summer of 2001 had its largest turnout to date: sixty attendees at the banquet, of whom slightly over 50% were women. Perhaps most interesting was that two of the female attendees were wives of customers.

Very unexpectedly seven months later, the man with the handle, Georgia Powers, shut down the community's website. "It's with great regret that this website has seen its final day," Georgia Powers wrote in his one page farewell, posted at the same URL (www.gppays.com) where the Georgia Powers Bordello Connection used to be. "I've considered several options, but in the end the only viable option was to just shut the site down. . . . As with most things in life there comes a time to move on, and for me and for this site that time has come."

No one knows what will happen to the CyberWhore Monger community. Several posters believe other new websites may hold the community together, such as www.nvbrothels.com and www.sex-in-nevada.com. Others are skeptical. But Bashful says he's "still interested in Nevada's brothels and will continue working to contribute to the community." His latest endeavor is a new pricing survey of legal Nevada prostitutes' services. Whether Bashful ever decides to work on developing his social life outside the brothel world remains to be seen; he has yet to date a square and, in his own estimation, "still needs to lose weight."

Gone but not forgotten, Mustang Ranch still generates and perpetuates its mystique with the public. A Mustang Ranch liquor decanter that once cost $25 at the brothel's pink souvenir booth situated in the parking lot sold on eBay to a bidder in California for $96.59. And George receives weekly telephone calls from community activists nationwide who are interested in legalizing prostitution in their towns—cities such as San Francisco, San Diego, Portland, and West Hollywood. However, calls like these have come in for decades and nothing's changed—Nevada still remains the only state in America with legalized brothels.

ACKNOWLEDGMENTS

I would like to thank the people who enabled me to write this book:

Robert Hatcher, my mentor, who encouraged me to conduct and offered to sponsor a public health study among Nevada's licensed prostitutes. Without his unwavering support, I believe my determination to get inside Nevada's brothel industry would have been shaken long before I gained admittance.

James Trussell, who first brought his expertise to my brothel condom research and then loaned me a laptop to aid me in the writing of this book.

David Lee Warner and Charles Bennett, whose contributions to my brothel condom research were both appreciated and essential.

Malcolm Freeman and Ronald Chez, who urged me from the sidelines to take a break from medical school and write a nonacademic, nonfiction book about my experiences inside Nevada's brothels.

Harvard Medical School and the University of Washington School of Medicine's Children's Hospital and Regional Medical Center, which each supported me in my nonmedical endeavors. I am deeply grateful to a few individuals in particular:

Audrey Bernfield, Dan Goodenough, Daniel Federman, Nancy Oriol, Paul Farmer, Susan Marshall, Richard Shugerman, and Bruder Stapleton.

Cindy Klein Roche and John Taylor Williams, my literary agents, the former who found me, and the latter who watched over me like a nurturing father, teaching me the ropes of publication and never holding back on encouragement and praise.

Scott Moyers, my patient and astute editor, who rigorously challenged me to find my voice—through draft after draft—until my story finally emerged.

Beth Pearson, Sunshine Lucas, Sally Marvin, and Carol Schneider of Random House, who all helped to tidy up loose ends and spiff up this book on the home stretch before sharing it with the world.

My two research assistants: Glynis Hull-Rochelle, who transcribed and e-mailed from Prague hundreds of hours of taped interviews at a whirlwind pace; and Jennifer Nash, who immersed herself in the material and became almost as obsessed as me.

Amy Bach, Laurie Mittenthal, Aimee Crow, Hilary Levine, Rebecca Fletcher, Tanya Krasikov, Kara Dukakis, Hallie Stosur, and Roxanne Brame, friends who listened to my excitement and insecurities about this book incessantly for years. I would also like to thank other supportive friends: Cecile Delafield, Susie Hobbins, Amanda Peppercorn, Andrew Shapiro, Jon Rubin, Jody Dushay, Ellen Reid, Heather Hardy, and Etsu Taniguchi.

Ed Reading, Ben Wallace, Steven Sack, Diana Graham,

Larry Rand, and Laika Gelman, who read drafts in various stages and offered invaluable criticism and enthusiasm.

Senator and Mrs. Len Nevin, Senator and Mrs. Raymond Shaffer, Assemblyman Bob Price, Ellen Pillard, George Williams III, Alberta Nelson, Bette Flint, Guy Louis Rocha and Jeff Kintop of the Nevada State Library and Archives, Randall Todd and Bob Nellis of the Bureau of Disease Control and Intervention Services for the Nevada State Health Division, Bob Cowan and Kim Raines of the Washoe County Library–Reno Periodicals Department, and Tisha Johnson of the State of Nevada Uniform Crime Reporting Program, who kindly shared their knowledge and perspectives with me.

Kassie Evashevski, Jonny King, Olivier Sultan, Noah Tratt, Susannah Lang-Hollister, Deborah Yokoe, Hope Denekamp, Milan Ganik, and Amelia Zalcman, who all performed small favors that made a big difference.

Mary Ruby and Rosemary DeCroce, who helped keep me sane and reminded me of what I was capable of both becoming and creating.

Monica Rose-Ziglar, who allowed me to finish this book by caring for my baby daughter with tenderness and affection.

Mike Sack and John Saul, who generously shared their experience and wisdom as professional writers.

Lynn and Burt Sack, my in-laws, who looked out for my husband when I was living in Nevada and continued to love me despite my unconventional pursuits.

Vera Brown, my great-aunt, who has been my guardian angel.

Marvin Albert, my father, who taught me the value of dreaming big and the art of working passionately.

Judy Albert, my mother, who obliged my requests as a child to drive past the streetwalkers who lined the doorways of Seattle's First Avenue peepshows and porn theaters. Her openness, curiosity, and compassion for others are three of the most important gifts she has given me.

My daughter, Coco, who waited patiently in utero as I tried to finish my last draft.

There are three debts that are unpayable.

I owe the first to George Flint, executive director of the Nevada Brothel Association, without whom this book would never have been written. Thank you for trusting me and for opening the doors to this exotic world.

I owe the second to the many individuals who shared themselves with me and whose stories helped to inform this book. I wish I could acknowledge you all by name. Thank you for letting me into your lives. I hope you feel I have done justice to your experiences. Most especially, I wish to thank the prostitutes of Mustang Ranch, whom I will always remember with the deepest respect, fondness, and awe.

I owe the greatest debt to my husband, Andy Sack. Thank you for respecting my desire and need to write this book. You are my lifeboat, my confidant, my comedian, my lover, and my best friend.

ALEXA ALBERT is a graduate of Brown University and Harvard Medical School. She has written and lectured widely on issues of public health and prostitution and was named one of *Mirabella*'s 1,000 Women for the Nineties for her work with Nevada's legal prostitutes. She currently lives with her husband and daughter in Seattle, where she is completing her pediatric residency.